IN HONOR OF THE HOLY SPIRIT

CASH LUNA

IN HONOR OF THE HOLY SPIRIT

He is someone, not something!

The mission of Editorial Vida is to be the leader in Christian communications, meeting the needs of people by providing resources that glorify Jesus Christ and promote biblical principles.

IN HONOR OF THE HOLY SPIRIT
Published in English by
Editorial Vida – 2012
Miami, Florida

Translation: *Words for the World*
Edited: *Full Well Ventures*
Revised by: *Elmer García, Jacob Lee Boyd, Jason Patton, Teresa Patton, Paola Pantaleón*
Interior design: *Gustavo A. Camacho*

ISBN: 978-0-8297-5997-6

CATEGORY: Christian Life/General

PRINTED IN THE UNITED STATES OF AMERICA

12 13 14 15 ❖ 6 5 4 3 2 1

I WOULD LIKE TO THANK...

Sonia, my wife and faithful friend, who has always been with me carrying out everything that we have believed God for.

My children, who lovingly supported me whenever Jesus calls me to travel to the nations taking His Word and His power, knowing that I would not see them for many days so that I can be a blessing to others. Today they love the Lord and serve Him together with me.

My mother, for believing in me as a child when I would tell her that I wanted to be a missionary and assuring me that I would achieve my goal even though neither of us knew what that would mean.

My awesome team, the greatest gift that God has given me in my ministry after His Holy Spirit. Thanks to them, their diligent work and unconditional support, I have been able to go to the places that God has taken me.

The members of "Casa de Dios" (House of God) church that I founded and now serve as Senior Pastor, for the love and respect that they have shown me and my family.

DEDICATION

TO THE HOLY SPIRIT, member of the Trinity, whom I deeply love. I am very grateful for all of His patience towards me.

CONTENTS

INTRODUCTION

During my childhood I learned a lot of lessons about Jesus. I learned that He did miracles, healed the sick, walked on water, multiplied the loaves and the fish, and also gave Himself as a sacrifice for our salvation.

Even though as a child I had learned a number of lessons about the Lord Jesus, it was not until July 11, 1982, that I came to know Him as my personal Lord and Savior. It was on that day I was born again. His grace reached me.

Ever since that moment, more than twenty-five years ago, I have never ceased serving Him with my utmost devotion, continually sharing my testimony, just as the apostles did during their ministry here on earth.

I waited a long time to write my first book because I understood that it takes time to develop a mature relationship with the Holy Spirit, just as it does with any other person. When I received His power and He began to use me to make His presence and His miracles known to others, I felt a great desire to write about him. In fact, I drafted the first chapter of this book ten years before it was published, but I put it on hold for a while to meditate. I realized that it would be more sensible to wait until I felt sure that I could maintain a close relationship with the Holy Spirit and retain the supernatural power I had received in my life.

In your hands you now have a book containing unique life lessons that you will not find in other publications on this subject. I am certain that this combination of teachings and stories about my personal life experiences will edify your life and motivate you to seek His presence and desire a closer relationship with Him more than anything else He can give you.

If, after you finish reading this book, you feel a greater hunger and thirst for God, then my purpose in writing it will have been fulfilled.

— Cash Luna

Chapter 1

I Awaken, and I Am Still with You

There are moments in life that tend to make a man nervous, for example, a final exam for a university course or facing your in-laws to request the hand of your sweetheart. I well remember how nervous I felt the day I first met the love of my life! I felt butterflies going wild in my stomach! I was uncertain of how to act or what to say, and when I finally thought I had just the right words, with a tremble in my voice, I said the first thing that popped into my mind and then fell silent. My mind suddenly went blank and soon I found that the great conversation I had pictured having, lasted only a few minutes.

And what about the wedding day? We men always seem to forget something important, or worse yet, we may remember during our honeymoon that we forgot to invite a friend to the ceremony. Another event that tends to make us very nervous is the birth of our first child. In my own case, I remember planning every last detail with my wife's doctor. My plan was to be present during the childbirth, but when the moment came to go into the delivery room, the doctor saw how nervous I was. So he simply squeezed my hand and gently pushed me aside, saying: "See you later." Next thing you know, he just disappeared and left me standing there in the hallway.

The truth is that every person is bound to experience life-changing moments, but we will not all react in the same way. Only on a few occasions have I been quite as nervous as I was on a certain memorable day in August of 1994. I was about to enter one of the most important churches to enjoy one of its famous revival meetings. For more than eleven years I had prayed for a greater awakening in my own life. I had been seeking the Lord's presence and His anointing with all my heart when I heard news that the power of God was being poured out with great intensity in those revival meetings to such a degree that it could even be felt in the parking lot. I had great expectations. I believed that the moment I walked through the door, the Holy Spirit would come upon me and leave me stretched out on the floor. I had imagined that when I rose to my feet again I would be the most anointed man that ever lived.

When I was finally seated, I felt very disappointed. The power of the Lord was real in that place; it would be foolish to deny it. The Holy Spirit was touching many people but nothing was happening to me. At least I did not seem to be experiencing what most were.

At times I felt a slight tingling in my skin, but that was all. After going to those meetings for several days, twelve to be precise, I was beyond frustration. Nothing had happened to me even though I had attended meetings twice every day, an average of seven hours per day.

Can you imagine? Praying over eleven years, maintaining a life of holiness, serving the Lord, and then nothing happening! Many questions flooded my mind. I could not doubt that the power of God was present there, but I also could not say that I had personally experienced it.

When the preacher gave an altar call for those who wanted to receive the anointing, in other words, the power of God, I would race to the front of the line. After the prayer, while everyone else had fallen under God's power, I would still be standing there. I should also point out that my wife was constantly being filled with the power of the Holy Spirit. Every night, with the best of intentions, she would try to explain to me how she had received the power of God and tried to motivate me to do the same. Sonia was drinking so deeply from the rivers of God that on one occasion, after stepping out of our car to go into the church, I noticed that she was not carrying her Bible. I asked her why since she always made a habit of taking it with her, not only because she was a Christian, but also because she was a pastor's wife and wanted to set a good example. Smiling back, she answered: "Today I am going to drink so much of the Holy Spirit that you will have to carry me out in your arms."

As a matter of fact, during that meeting Sonia experienced God's power and she was completely filled with His presence. Her experience was so over-whelming that while she was lying on the carpet I approached her, moved her a little and said: "Did your blood pressure drop suddenly, honey?" She slowly turned her head and gave me such a stern look that I can assure you that at that moment I received the gift of interpretation of glances and I thought to myself: "I'd better go out and get a cup of coffee."

A little while later I did end up carrying my wife who was overflowing with God's presence. Obviously,

17

faced with such unavoidable evidence, my frustration increased to the point that one day, while seated on one of the steps of the church building, I began to sob like a child who had lost his closest friend. Then I asked God why I was not receiving the powerful anointing that other people had. I reminded God that I was a man of prayer who devoted more than one hour daily to communing with Him; I fasted and consistently sought to live a life of holiness.

That is when God confronted me: "Carlos, your problem is faith," said the Lord. "But," I responded, "I am a person who others regard as a man of faith." "Look at yourself," said the Lord. "You have money in the bank, but you don't even have the faith to enjoy buying yourself a good pair of shoes".

At that moment, God challenged me and changed my attitude. "If you do not have the faith to get a pair of shoes, how can you expect to have the faith to see My glory? Which is greater, My glory or a new pair of shoes?"

I sincerely thought twice about including this experience in the book, but I decided I could not leave it out. Although it may sound ridiculous, that simple question changed my entire life.

The Bible is full of stories about God sending people to do some very strange things. I believe this fact encouraged me and enabled me to follow through. Think about this for a moment: If we do not have faith for material things, how can we have the faith for spiritual ones? If I

If we do not have faith for material things, how can we have faith for spiritual ones?

18

do not have faith for the little things, how can I have the faith for bigger ones?

In my experience, God confronted me before He anointed me. I understood that without faith it is impossible to please God, so the next day I put my faith into practice in everything I did, including, of course, getting myself a new pair of shoes. That night the miracle happened. I had asked the senior pastor of the church if the guest minister could pray for me that following Sunday during the service. The pastor willingly obliged. However, that night the Holy Spirit said to me: "You already got what you desire; you can go home now."

I believed Him and decided to go home even though I had not yet experienced anything very powerful. That night after my wife and I had gone to bed and were lying there, I closed my eyes to get some rest when I slowly began to feel that I was being covered with a blanket or comforter. At first I thought it was my wife covering me up. Then I felt like another blanket was placed over me, and another and another, until I literally began to sink in my bed under the weight. Finally, I opened my eyes to see what was happening and was surprised to find no extra blankets on me; in fact, I had nothing over me except a very light sheet, yet my wife and I were both sinking into the mattress due to the extra weight on us!

I looked at my wife and said: "Sonia, it's Him; He's doing this." She smiled and replied: "Yes, it is Him." In effect, it was the weight of His power, His very presence that was manifesting on us. That powerful anointing that I had sought out for years on end did not come when someone prayed over me, but rather when I simply believed God with all my heart.

Since that time, I've experienced the glorious presence of the Holy Spirit in my life and ministry. His strength has constantly been with me to this day. His visitation was so intense that I couldn't sleep for entire nights. His presence wrapped me up like a soft yet heavy mantle charged with power. It felt like a tangible presence, like a weight upon me and a strong electric current that ran through my entire body. His Word flooded my mind for hours like a showering rain of verses that transformed me. Hours would go by until from my bedroom window I could see the sun's first rays, and the words from Psalm 139:18 became a reality in my life: "When I awaken, I am still with you."

The best part is that ever since that special day I have not ceased to experience the power of the Holy Spirit in my life and ministry. More than fifteen years have passed and each day I still feel as fresh and new as that night. It is wonderful to know that the presence of God in whom I have believed, has manifested Himself without reservation and that I can spend entire nights with Him, praying until dawn.

Even now I sense Him filling me with His sweet and gentle presence and I pray that after you read this simple yet profound book, your life will never be the same. Your hunger and thirst for His presence will lead you to seek Him with your entire being.

Right there, where you are at this moment, He wants to fill you. In your bedroom or perhaps your office, in a restaurant sipping a cup of coffee, or on an airplane as you travel. No matter where you may be, whether you are going

The Lord desires you more than you could ever desire Him in all your life.

through a trial or just getting ready for work, He is longing to visit you.

His Word teaches us that His Spirit, whom He has sent to live in us, "desires us intensely" (James 4:5). The Lord desires you more than you could ever desire Him in all your life. The Holy Spirit desires that you seek Him, that you take time to be alone with Him, with no one else around. More than that, He wants to be in fellowship with you, even in public. God wants you to be attentive to His voice, listening to His leading, His guidance and His direction even when you are talking with other people.

Nights of Glory

Our church had only been open for three months and we were still meeting at a hotel in Guatemala City. There were times when people were unable to enter our meeting halls because the powerful presence of the Lord had filled the lobby, the hallways and even the restrooms. Eventually the hotel administration would not allow us to continue holding meetings there because Sunday mornings we ended up having more people drunk in the Holy Spirit than they had in their parties every Friday and Saturday night.

In December of that year I felt moved by the Holy Spirit to set aside six consecutive nights to minister the Word and the power of God to all those who desired Him. The price for renting out the hotel hall would be too expensive, so I asked a friend who oversaw the World Harvest Bible School to rent us their main hall to hold the meetings there. He immediately accepted our request.

We had not given the meetings any special name nor had we done any advertising about them. The in-

21

vitation was simply by word of mouth, until a young person showed me a small flyer with the words "Nights of Glory" on it. Thus, informally, yet inspired by God, the meetings began that are now known by that name. They provided a venue where people thirsty for His presence could experience times of refreshing, a place to drink of the wine of the Holy Spirit and receive great miracles while growing in the knowledge of our Lord Jesus Christ. The lives of those people who attended, full of faith, were changed never again to be the same.

Because of the anointing of the Holy Spirit and the growing number of testimonies of people touched by God, those evening meetings began to grow until becoming great healing crusades of miracles and anointing.

It is wonderful to minister when one is anointed. Sometimes miracles begin to occur through His power alone, without even needing to say a word. An example of this is what happened at a healing crusade that we held in Loja, a small city in Ecuador. In that city there were perhaps eight Christian churches, but ninety percent of those attending the Nights of Glory meetings at the Coliseum were not born-again Christians.

The first night of that great crusade there was light drizzling rain. Nonetheless, the people came and the place was completely packed. Many were expecting a miracle from Jesus, and many of them would have an encounter they would never forget. The service was lovely, although we had to teach almost every song we sang because hardly anyone knew them. Everyone raised their hands when invited to do so and their voices filled that entire place. The worship was truly beautiful. Tears come to my eyes every time I remember that evening. I was completely given over to God in worship when suddenly the shouts of a woman interrupted the meeting. She was standing on the steps to the left of the platform. At first I thought she was trying to disrupt the meeting, and wanting to restore order the way I thought was the best, I asked one of the members of our team to find out what was happening. Then I began to hear clearly what the woman was shouting: "I was blind! I was blind! I was blind!"

Jesus had done it again. He had done according to His will. He healed the woman without asking anyone's permission. He did not wait for a preplanned moment. He did not follow the rules, nor even tell me what He was doing. He just did it! That woman who wasn't even saved had instantly recovered her sight. Jesus healed her.

She probably did not know anything about religious formalities, so she did not wait for a specific moment to experience her miracle. It simply happened while she was praising the Lord. A light appeared in front of her and she prayed: "My eye! Jesus, my eye!" Then she felt a fire go through her blind eye and immediately she could see again. The entire Coliseum burst into shouts of praise and gave our Lord Jesus all the honor and the glory.

The Power of the Anointing

It is impossible to minister without the anointing. When God's Spirit descends, the whole atmosphere changes and things happen that would not occur if He had not manifested Himself. A man of God once said: "I cannot define the anointing, but I definitely know when it is there and when it is not." Another minister defined the anointing as "the manifest power of God."

In fact, almost all definitions given of Him are very similar. I believe the anointing is the power of the Holy Spirit in a person's life designed to accomplish the supernatural work of God. In the end, it's not a matter of how to define it, but of how to receive it. What is important is not learning about it, but rather accepting it. The difficult part is not receiving it, but retaining it.

Many people have prayed throughout their entire lives seeking to enjoy the anointing and sincerely confess they have not experienced it, or they at least admit they have not seen tangible results. Others have had a supernatural experience and received the anointing but have been unable to retain it. Others go from conference to conference and attend many church services seeking to renew their experience, because they have been unable to retain it in their own personal walk and ministry. Worse yet, there are those who believe that the anointing means to be overly emotional when preaching, to shout or scream and perspire excessively.

The anointing has nothing to do with one's personal style of doing things. The anointing is the essence of the Holy Spirit's power manifested on a person's life. It is not a dove flapping its wings, seeking to enter your life and resting upon you as if by magic or some religious trick. The anointing comes and remains on you when you

The anointing is the essence of the Holy Spirit's power manifested on a person's life.

genuinely and diligently seek God and His power. The Bible tells us in Psalm 105:4-5: "Look to the Lord and his strength; seek his face always. Remember the wonders He has done, His miracles, and the judgments He has pronounced."

We must seek the Lord as a *person*, that is, as someone with whom we can enjoy an intimate relationship. We should seek His face and His power as well. If you focus more intently on the Scripture above, you will notice that the psalmist is reminding the people of the marvels and wonders of the Lord. Beyond that, he exhorts them to seek His face and power if they desire to see them manifested. Even the revealed Word, what some refer to as the *Rhema* Word of God (that Word given to a specific person, for a specific purpose, at a specific moment in time), will come if we seek His presence, since that is the only way we can hear His voice to reveal His will at any given time.

Being anointed is not a question of luck or accident. The anointing is for those who seek the Lord, His face and His power. You will sense it upon your life as a direct result of diligently, passionately and sincerely seeking for His presence. While it is true that Jesus paid the price on the cross at Calvary, and we experience it by the Lord's grace, it is also true that He never gives it to those who do not value it. As a matter of fact, some have even lost it for that reason.

If you are reading this book it is because you desire with all your heart to receive His anointing, retain it and allow it to grow in your life and ministry. My dear friend, there is something beyond the anointing, and that is exactly what I want to show you now.

CHAPTER 2

Beyond My Understanding

Some years ago my wife and I went on a retreat for married couples. The two friends with whom we shared a cabin talked to us about the temperaments that psychologists describe as characteristics typically present from birth. According to these studies, there are four basic types of temperaments which are: sanguine, choleric, melancholic, and phlegmatic. While they were explaining each of them to us, I identified my own temperament as a combination of two different types.

At that time they gave us a test to identify these personality profiles and my thoughts were confirmed: two of them were dominant in my life, considerably more than the others. When I heard of the advantages of each one, I was encouraged to read about the positive traits, but I was disappointed to learn of their weaknesses. My first thought was: "With traits like these, I will never get anywhere."

That night I could not sleep thinking that my whole life would be doomed by the weaknesses of my temperament. I wanted to serve the Lord in His strength, not mine. I did not want to boast in achieving success through my own natural abilities, nor did I want to end up frustrated by failure due to my own shortcomings.

I asked myself what role the Holy Spirit would play in our lives if we were going to live according to our temperaments. If I accepted that my human weaknesses were impossible to overcome or if I sought to hide behind my personality, it would keep the Holy Spirit from working His transformation in me.

I imagined myself on the day that I would give an account before God, trying to excuse myself on the basis of my personality type, telling God that was the reason why I did not do the things that I should have done. How could I tell God that I did not do what He commanded me to because I was fearful by nature, or that I had a hard time forgiving others because my temperament was that of a person prone to be resentful all the time? How could I tell God that I reached all my goals, but at the expense of stepping all over everyone else? How could I ever tell Him that I got distracted along the way because my temperament rarely allowed me to finish what I started? That was inconceivable in my mind and that is why I refused to live that way.

Then I made a decision which would be one of the most important of my life. I decided to submit my personality type to the obedience of the Holy Spirit. I thought that if I were predisposed to depend only on my strengths and weaknesses, I would live by the strength of my flesh and not seek and depend on the Holy Spirit to enable me to bear fruit. I would be assuming that my weaknesses could not be corrected and that no transforming work would be possible in my life. Therefore I believed that the fruit produced by the Holy Spirit in my life, including love, patience, meekness or temperance, surely all of these together would be able to overcome any weaknesses in my personality type. Thus every time I faced the reality of one of my weaknesses, I would surrender that area of my life to the Lord. When I presented my weaknesses to Him, He never rejected me saying: "You cannot do that because you have a tendency to get distracted," or "I cannot choose you to do that great work because your personality type never finishes what it starts."

Years later I retook the test and the results were that the four temperaments had been balanced in my life. This is the fruit of having submitted my behavior day in and day out to the Holy Spirit, so as to form new habits that have overcome most of my weaknesses. It was wonderful to confirm that the Holy Spirit is able to help us in our weaknesses and make us the people that He wants us to become!

It was wonderful to confirm that the Holy Spirit is able to help us in our weaknesses and make us the people that He wants us to become!

The Lord teaches us in the parable of the talents of a man who sought to justify himself before his lord for having buried the talent he had been entrusted with. He said: "I was afraid," meaning that he was dominated, not by adultery or fornication or a filthy lifestyle, but simply by fear.

You don't have to commit lustful deeds, heresy, adultery or fornication to be fleshly. It is enough to let your fallen nature have its way in your life. If you try to serve God on the basis of your human nature, you will wind up excusing yourself for your failures and weaknesses. If you say that your personality type is your only strength as well as your weakness, then where is the power of the Holy Spirit in your life?

31

That kind of talk acknowledges that you are living in your own strength.

I cannot deny the existence of these temperaments. In fact, we have studied them to better understand and educate our own children. My wife Sonia has used them in certain teachings she has given. Yet I am sure that the Lord would not have accomplished the work that He has in our ministry had I not submitted the weaknesses of my carnal nature to the Holy Spirit. Instead of justifying them with a personality type, I decided to submit them in obedience to the Lord.

Transforming Power

One time while talking with my father-in-law, a man who has become a dear friend of mine, he told me the following story: One day, the leaders of a church were in the process of deciding whom to invite to minister at one of their meetings. One of them, an older man, insisted on inviting a young person who had demonstrated God's anointing on his life and through whom God was performing signs, wonders and miracles. He was so insistent that another member of the group became angry and said: "Why does it have to be that young person? You make it seem like he's got a monopoly on the Holy Spirit." To which the older man replied: "Certainly not, but the Holy Spirit's definitely got a monopoly on him."

After sharing the story with me, my father-in-law concluded by saying: "You can never have control of the Holy Spirit, but you can seek to be that young person whom the Holy Spirit is in control of."

Many people would like to be used by the Lord to transform the lives of others, but few are willing to be transformed by Him. There's no doubt in my mind that you are reading this book because you are interested in the anointing, but I must remind you that one of the adjectives commonly used to describe it is His "holy anointing." The anointing that transforms will only rest upon people who desire to be transformed, and not only upon those who want to be used to transform others. We need to understand that holiness is based on the faith that we have in the grace of Jesus Christ who is able to sanctify us.

> *The anointing that transforms will only rest upon people who desire to be transformed, and not only upon those who want to be used to transform others.*

It is wrong to interpret holiness as perfect behavior, free of defects and errors. That is not how it really is. To live in holiness means to surrender our will to fulfill the commands that God gives us and that transforms us more and more each day. If the Lord takes clay in His hands to make a vessel, from the moment He takes it, it is holy, because the word "holy" means "set apart for Him." God sets that clay apart to shape it. Some people believe that you need to be perfect for God to anoint you. That is not true of any person in the Bible. There was no prophet or apostle in all the Scriptures who was perfect, and certainly there are none today either. But there are those who have consecrated themselves to live in a constant state of transformation, just like clay in the potter's hands.

When the power of God is manifest in my life, some people may think I am perfect, but that really is not the case. I am far from achieving perfection, but the one thing I do is consecrate my life to God every day so that He may continue transforming me.

Psalm 139:1-6 tells us: "O Lord, you have searched me and you know me. You know when I sit and when I rise; you perceive my thoughts from afar. You discern my going out and my lying down; you are familiar with all my ways. Before a word is on my tongue you know it completely, O Lord. You hem me in — behind and before; you have laid your hand upon me. Such knowledge is too wonderful for me, too lofty for me to attain."

We cannot be transformed apart from His presence. God fills us hoping that we will become bearers of His holy anointing wherever we go. He gives us His Spirit not because we are holy but so that we can become holy. Without His presence it is impossible to achieve holiness.

When I read this Psalm for the first time I assumed that the thoughts, the words, the walk, the lying down and the rising up of that man were perfect, and that God had surrounded him for that reason. However, as I meditated on the Scripture and after years of being in His presence, I realized that I was mistaken. Meditate on these words for a moment. The psalmist said: "You hem me in — behind and before; you have laid your hand upon me. Such knowledge is too wonderful for me, too lofty for me to attain."

If this man were perfect in all his deeds, thoughts and emotions, the presence of God would have been completely natural for him; he would have felt that he deserved such a privilege, but that is not the case. I believe that he thought otherwise. He realized that no matter how good and righteous his behavior might be, it was never enough to experience the presence of God, and that is why he declares himself unworthy. His words might have been: "Lord, how is it that you surround me with Your presence and place Your hand upon me, knowing me as only you can know me? You know that I am not the best of Your children. You know that my thoughts are not always good and that my behavior is certainly not perfect."

An Intimate Encounter

Dear friend, the Lord knows your words even before they come out of your mouth. He knows your heart and every detail of your being, yet His hand is upon you and He has chosen to surround you with His presence. Isn't such knowledge wonderful and incomprehensible? He does not wait until you are perfect before overshadowing you; instead, He surrounds you in order to make you better. You do not have to be holy to receive Him. The presence of God helps you to become holy as He is holy.

You do not have to be holy to receive Him. The presence of God helps you to become holy, as He is holy.

Why do I believe this? Because in the following verses the Psalmist wrote: "Where can I go from your Spirit? Where can I flee from your presence? If I go up to the heavens, you are there; if I make my bed in the depths, you are there. If I rise on the wings of the dawn, if I settle on the far side of the sea, even there your hand will guide me, your right hand will hold me fast." (Psalm 139:7-10)

Now I ask you: Why would a man who is so righteous flee from the presence of God? Could it be that such a presence made him feel unworthy? In my case, the eleven years that I prayed and asked for the anointing does not begin to compare with what I received and now have. His desire to give me His anointing surpassed my greatest desire to have it. My time in prayer will never compare to the price that He paid on the cross. God wants to give you so much that anything that you do will always pale in comparison to His desire to anoint you. The anointing you receive from the Lord is not the product of anything that you might do to obtain it, but rather of His intense desire to give it to you. It is a treasure of untold value, He will give you the anointing only if you desire and appreciate it.

He wants to surround you and He will seek you out wherever you are. It doesn't matter how often you try to hide or flee from Him. There is no hiding place where He cannot find you. God is literally pursuing you in order to transform you. If you want His anointing in your life and ministry, the first thing you must do is allow His presence to flood you from head to toe and from inside out.

You should be sensitive and allow the presence of the Lord to mold you so that afterward you can receive the anointing that will help you change others. There is nothing more marvelous than to let the Holy Spirit work in us and transform us.

The prophet Isaiah experienced a transformation in the presence of God before he was able to say: "Here I am, Lord; send me." His mouth, his tongue, his whole being was changed before the glory of the Lord. It was in His presence that he felt like a dead man and his sin was revealed to him.

Here we clearly see the process again: The presence of God surrounded Isaiah and an angelic being came down from God's throne with a burning coal to transform him. God did not surround him because his conduct was perfect, but rather so that he might become perfect.

The people transformed by the Lord are people of prayer who maintain fellowship and intimacy with Him. They not only study the Word, but they also spend time in His presence. The one who seeks God so that his heart, his words, and his thoughts might be searched, recognizing his own need to be shaped and renewed, is the one who will experience a deeper transformation of his spirit.

> *The people transformed by the Lord are people of prayer who maintain fellowship and intimacy with Him.*

If you do not want the Spirit of God to change your life then you won't get to know Him very well either. You might have theoretical knowledge about the Holy Spirit, but you will not get to know Him in an intimate way. When you make your life transparent before Him, you'll submit yourself to a radical change in your manner of thinking, speaking and acting, in addition to experiencing first-hand the manifestation of His true nature. The more transparent you are to God with your spirit, the more He will reveal His to you. The more you open your heart to God, the more He will open His to you, for the Scripture says: Draw near to God and He will draw near to you.

This is the kind of prayer that helps you behold God in all His majesty. It's the one that is truly transformed, and not just goes through vain repetition of words. The true change starts the moment you bow at His feet and tell Him: "Lord, I am a person with a hard heart and You know it. I cannot hide it from You." When you come before His presence and say: "Lord, You know my life, You know what I do, You know every word I speak; here I am, change me," then that is when you open your life to a transformation that will gradually lead you to an intimate knowledge of His Spirit. He seeks intimacy with those who demonstrate a longing to find Him.

Though it might seem difficult to believe, you should not only think about how much you desire Him, but also about how much He desires you. That is why the Scriptures teach us that the Holy Spirit jealously yearns for us.

I remember one occasion when I asked the Lord to manifest Himself and to cause His power to descend upon the meetings and touch the people. I would always pray that this might happen. But one day the Holy Spirit spoke to me and said: "Today I'm going to descend with My power not because the people desire Me to, but because I long to do so." And He added: "Many have taught that they should desire Me, but few really understand how much I long for them." And He continued explaining: "When two people are in fellowship, the desire is mutual, and there is no greater desire than that which I have for you." To seek the Spirit is the beginning of an unimaginable relationship between you and Him.

If He desires us so much that He put it in writing, why don't we take advantage of that reality and desire Him ourselves. This two-way search and desire will produce a wonderful relationship: the love that we give Him and that we receive from Him.

Dear reader, even though you may be a success-ful person, a good student, a great businessman or professional, you need to achieve spiritual success as well. To see the glory of God reflected in your life is the ultimate success! Nothing can compare to it. Seek it out with all your heart!

CHAPTER 3

He Is Someone, Not Something

One night I suddenly awoke at three o'clock in the morning weeping uncontrollably. I had fallen asleep thinking about how to explain the manifestations of the power of God to those who might ask. When the presence of God is manifest, unusual things happen. For example, people may fall to the floor or tremble when divine power is poured upon them. It is difficult to understand the reason for the doubts and questions of those who observe this, since we humans are used to seeing our bodies react to material things, such as anesthesia. We're not surprised to see someone appearing dumbfounded, dazed and unable to speak as a result of some medication. The effects of things that are natural or chemical are accepted by our minds, and yet we find it so difficult to comprehend the effects brought about by the power of the Holy Spirit. With much sorrow I see some Christians who are ashamed of these manifestations of power. They feel so confused that they even try to hide these things to keep other people from feeling embarrassed or afraid.

That night I woke up weeping. I was not crying out of sorrow or thankfulness, but rather due to an overwhelming impression in my heart. I did not know where it came from, but I could feel the presence of the Holy Spirit before me saying: "Wherever you go, tell My people that I love them just as they are, with their virtues, strengths, defects, and weaknesses." After that there was a moment of silence and I started weeping even more intensely, knowing that He had not finished speaking to me. In effect, He continued, saying: "I want you to tell them to also accept Me just as I am, not as they would like Me to be, because I cannot change nor deny who I am."

Then my mind was filled with images of meetings I had ministered in. I saw the Holy Spirit approaching a person who could not withstand His Holy Presence and broke down weeping. Then I saw the Spirit approaching another person who was simply laughing out loud because a supernatural joy was flooding him. Another trembled, unable to withstand that great power. And as the Spirit approached the people, their bodies reacted under his power. Others, in the same meeting, grew uncomfortable and restless, critical of these manifestations. Later I felt as though He were looking at me and gently saying, "What do you want Me do? This is just how I am!"

That's when I understood that it's impossible to shake the hand of a heavyweight champion without feeling the grip of a hand that is stronger than normal, even though to him it is simply his natural strength. He cannot avoid pressing a hand forcefully because that is the way he is. To try to avoid the manifestations of the Holy Spirit would be like trying to approach a flower without smelling its aroma, or diving into water without getting

To try to avoid the manifestations of the Holy Spirit would be like trying to approach a flower without smelling its aroma.

wet, or passing your hand through fire and imagining you will not be burned. These things are unavoidable because the nature of those elements cannot be denied. In the same way, the Holy Spirit can't deny His nature just because some people do not understand Him. If He is able to accept us in spite of how we are, with our faults and weaknesses and all, then we should also accept Him just as He is. He's perfect!

His presence is powerful and we cannot avoid sensing it when He is around us or filling us. Wanting to avoid it is as naive as putting your finger in an electrical socket and imagining that the current won't shake your entire body. Electricity provokes a reaction in our bodies even if we do not know or understand how it works. The same is true of the manifestations of the power of God and they cause an effect in our bodies even when we do not fully understand them.

The Holy Spirit will never miss an opportunity to manifest Himself to you just out of fear of surprising you. If He did, He would not be Himself. Imagine if there were religious groups that did not practice the laying on of hands because people might fall to the ground and they wanted to avoid scaring new members away. With that attitude, Jesus would not have been able to raise Lazarus from the dead or walk on water. Imagine for a moment the disciples asking Him to be more discrete because spitting into mud and then putting it on the eyes of a blind man, or multiplying the loaves and fish would just be too scandalous. Perhaps they would say: "Careful Jesus, remember that they want to make You king. They think You are a politician and that is why You feed everyone. Don't You think we should carry on the ministry a little more discretely?" I would not dare to suggest such a thing to Jesus nor to the Holy Spirit. We must remember that He is the Lord and we are only His servants. I would prefer failure to limiting any of His power.

The Holy Spirit cannot deny Himself. We need to learn to know and accept Him just as He is, and not as we would prefer Him to be. This way we will recognize Him at any given moment. We should ask the Lord for forgiveness if we have criticized the Holy Spirit with our small and limited minds. Do not try to understand the power of God that manifests in so many strange ways, as with the parting of the Red Sea, the bringing down of the walls of Jericho or the raising of the dead. We cannot expect the Holy Spirit to act or think as a human being because He is not one of us, He is God Himself! We need to respect and love His personality in order to properly relate and commune with Him.

The Third Person

Who is the third person of the Trinity? Every time I ask that question, people tell me that it is the Holy Spirit, because that is what we were taught as children. It is true that the Holy Spirit is one of the three persons that make up the Trinity, but He does not necessarily occupy the third place. Nowhere in the Bible does it say this.

Even so, in the minds of most people, the Holy Spirit comes in third place because we have a mistaken idea engraved in our heads. The problem of being "the third person" is that no one pays attention to those who are in the third place of anything. Ask who won a competition and many will probably remember the winner. Some may even remember who came in second, but few, if any, remember who came in third.

The Holy Spirit does not occupy the third place in the Trinity. He is just as important as the Father and the Son, since the three are one. When we say that the Holy Spirit is the third person of the Trinity, we automatically relegate Him to third place in importance when that really is not the case. You cannot have a good relationship with the Holy Spirit if you do not render Him the importance He deserves. Your fellowship with Him will be much better when you value Him as the divine person that He is.

> The Holy Spirit does not occupy the third place in the Trinity. He is just as important as the Father and the Son, since the three are one.

Typically, when we hear about the Holy Spirit, our minds think of objects that we tend to associate with Him, as if He were "something" and not "someone." We think of Him as a dove because that is the form He took when He descended upon Jesus during His baptism, or we think of Him as fire because we remember the flames over the heads of the disciples on the day of Pentecost. But the Holy Spirit is not a dove and He is not fire; He is a person of the Deity with whom you can have a personal relationship. He makes us drunk as with wine but He is not wine; He anoints with oil but He is not oil; He is gentle as a breeze but He is not wind; and He fills us with rivers of life but He is not water. The Holy Spirit is a divine person, not a natural one.

He speaks to us, He listens, He teaches, and He desires to fellowship with us. He guides us, He reminds us of the Word, He sanctifies us and He intercedes for us. He can be resisted and quenched; He can be angered or saddened. We cannot study Him systematically, for we cannot explain a person like we do a simple concept. For example, it would be useless for me to try to study all the qualities of my wife Sonia without having fellowship with her. In like manner, it would be useless to try to understand everything about the Holy Spirit if I do not enjoy His presence. He is supernatural. More than study Him we need to know Him, and to do that we must have intimate fellowship with Him.

To be baptized in the Holy Spirit and speak in other tongues does not automatically mean that you know Him. Knowing all His attributes and qualities does not necessarily lead to greater intimacy. Just as when you are in a relationship with another person, you must spend time with that person to know him. The most important thing in our lives should be to walk in the presence of God. His companionship is worth more than anything else in this life. For that reason, the Lord has given us the Holy Spirit to accompany us wherever we go. It is He who gives us the power of God.

The Importance of the Holy Spirit

The entire Bible reveals the importance of the Holy Spirit in creation, in the prophets, in the life of Jesus and the development of the Early Church. It was He who conceived Jesus in Mary's womb. His fullness was the first thing given to John the Baptist when both he and Jesus were still in their mothers' wombs. Elizabeth felt the baby leap for joy in her womb and was filled with the Holy Spirit upon hearing the voice of Mary. Jesus was not yet born when the Holy Spirit had already been manifested through Him. The first recorded statement that John the Baptist said about our Lord was that He would baptize in the Holy Spirit and with fire. The following day John referred to Him as "the Lamb that takes away the sins of the world," signaling that the baptism in the Spirit is as important as redemption from our sins. John the Baptist recognized that Jesus was the Messiah because he saw the Holy Spirit descend like a dove upon His head and remain upon Him.

When Jesus was baptized in water, He heard the voice of His Father from heaven and saw the Holy Spirit come upon Him in the form of a dove. Immediately afterwards, in Luke 4:1, we are told: "Jesus, full of the Holy Spirit, returned to the Jordan, and was led by the Spirit into the wilderness." After going into the desert and overcoming temptations, in Luke 4:14 we read: "Jesus returned to Galilee in the power of the Spirit, and his fame was extended throughout the region." That is to say, Jesus' fame grew due to the power of the Holy Spirit.

During Jesus ministry, He healed the sick and cured infirmities because the Spirit had anointed Him. He also declared to the Pharisees that if it were by the Spirit that He cast out demons, it was because the kingdom of God had come near them. Do you know what the subject was of the first message Jesus preached in the synagogue? That's right; it was on the Holy Spirit!

During the last supper, on the day He would be arrested, Jesus gave instructions to His disciples. Many of these were about the work of the Holy Spirit, including His assurance that it was better for Him to leave so that the Comforter would come. When Jesus died,

He offered Himself up through the eternal Spirit and rose again by the same power.

Before ascending to heaven He appeared to His disciples over a period of forty days, giving them commands and telling them of the promise of the Father to baptize them very soon in the Holy Spirit.

On the day of Pentecost they were filled with the Holy Spirit, as tongues of fire appeared over their heads. At that moment, the apostle Peter stood up and gave the first message in the history of the Christian Church. What was the subject of the first sermon preached? The Holy Spirit! He said: "Fellow Jews and all of you who live in Jerusalem, let me explain this to you; listen carefully to what I say. These men are not drunk, as you suppose. It's only nine in the morning! No, this is what was spoken by the prophet Joel: 'In the last days, God says, I will pour out my Spirit upon all people'" (Acts 2:14-17a).

Then he spoke of Jesus as the one sent by God to save the world. During the message some people whose hearts were contrite accepted Jesus as their Savior, and immediately they were given the gift promised by God: the Holy Spirit.

His presence was the most important thing in the Early Church. We read in the book of Acts again and again of how the Holy Spirit was manifested. They prayed for everyone to be baptized in the Holy Spirit. They ministered in His power; the fullness of the Holy Spirit was even a requirement for future deacons! But now the opposite is all too common. We have minimized His importance and He is among the last things that we talk about in our meetings. He is apparently only important for all-night prayer vigils, baptisms and the impartation of gifts. That is so not right. We should return to the ancient paths, to the path that was taken by Jesus and His disciples. It's the path in which the first thing to recognize is His presence.

If you have minimized or looked down on the importance of the Holy Spirit in your life, you should ask God to forgive you. If you have grown cold and adopted a bad attitude toward God and the Holy Spirit, this is a good time to return to Him again.

There is no reason for you to turn away from the Lord; you gain nothing by departing from His way and from the presence of the Holy Spirit. The key to every move of God is in understanding and believing in the importance of the Holy Spirit as the divine person that He is and that you walk according to that conviction.

The key to every move of God is in understanding and believing in the importance of the Holy Spirit as the divine person that He is and that you walk according to that conviction.

Be honest with yourself and reasonable in your actions. God has never done anything wrong to you to cause you to turn your back on Him. On the contrary, He has had more than enough patience with you, He has blessed you, He has always loved you, and He has defended you. The Holy Spirit is always with you and He is your Comforter. He anoints and fills you with His strength and power.

Fellowship and Intimacy

Some time ago, while I was still single, I went through a very difficult financial trial. Because of that I had to

51

stop going to College, although years later I would be able to finish and graduate. At that time, for reasons beyond my control, I was left without a place to live. On the day I was to leave the house where I was staying at, not knowing where I would go or where I would sleep that night, I said to God, "I'm going to go to church to worship you without worrying about where I'm going to sleep, knowing that You will provide for me."

I worshiped the Lord with all my heart that night at the meeting, and the peace of God overwhelmed me. At the end of the service, a friend came to me and invited me for dinner at his grandmother's home. The first thing that came to mind was: "God has already provided me with somewhere to eat." After lunch, my friend told me that I could stay at his house, but the only place they had was a small room with a rug. I jumped for joy because I now had a roof over my head for the night! When we were saying goodbye to his grandmother, she told me she had something to show me and then took me to a storage room in the back of the house and showed me a foldaway bed, similar to a "cot." She asked if I wanted it so I would not have to sleep on the carpet, to which I said yes with all the gratitude of my heart. Even though it was moldy, with a dank and musty smell, after a little cleaning it was wonderful. That's the moment that I felt I had begun to prosper in God! He did not leave me sleeping on the floor, for I now had a bed. I understood there and then that even if I could afford to get the best bed in the world, I could not buy the sleep and rest that only the Lord could give me.

For many people such loneliness can be lethal; they are filled with sorrow and spend all their time complaining. But in my case, the time I could spend alone with God in that bedroom was something to look forward to.

At that time, Sonia and I were already engaged. I would visit her every day after work, and from there I would head back to my friend's house, where I was living. I remember all too well what time I'd usually leave because it was around the same time a Christian radio station started its programming in English. I would take advantage of the long trip back home to worship and meditate on the Word of God through that program. What I mostly looked forward to was getting back to that small bedroom and enjoying being alone in His presence.

A friend kindly loaned me a very special guitar. It was smaller than a normal one and it had a missing string. The remaining five strings were out of tune. Since I am not a musician I did not know how to tune it, but I didn't care. So it was in that small room, with an out-of-tune guitar and my off-key voice, that I took advantage of my time alone to worship God, not knowing that He was preparing me to walk in His power. It was there in that time alone with Him that I learned to seek Him.

Throughout that experience I learned that if the Holy Spirit is with us, we are never alone. How sad it must be for Him, being our companion, hearing us complain about how lonely we feel! If He is with you, you should never complain nor even feel alone.

That is how I first got to know the Holy Spirit in a deep way. In that solitude I learned to know "the One who can do all things." I meditated, prayed and sang to Him. It was beautiful! Today I remember those times as one of the most precious seasons of my life. One can learn to know God so well in intimate settings. Thank you Lord for that blessed solitude with You! Learn to take advantage of your moments alone. These times often are the key for developing an intimate relationship with the person of the Holy Spirit.

Learn to take advantage of your moments alone. These times often are the key for developing an intimate relationship with the person of the Holy Spirit.

Many people want to be filled with the Holy Spirit but not led by Him. Jesus was led into the wilderness to be alone in intimacy with Him and to receive His power. There are some who do not believe that the Spirit can lead them through a wilderness because they automatically associate that with something bad. He takes you by the hand and leads you through moments of solitude and loneliness so that you may come to know Him better. When you are going through a wilderness, do not belittle the Spirit by griping about how lonely you feel, because He will never leave you. He will always be there with you to help you, just as He was with Jesus.

If you have been filled with the presence of the Holy Spirit, allow yourself to be led by Him. Being filled with and walking with the Holy Spirit are two different things. There is a wilderness between them. This is where you must learn to be alone with Him so that He may invite you to know Him and walk in His power, because it is impossible to walk in the power of someone you do not know.

The apostle Paul wrote: "May the grace of the Lord Jesus Christ, and the love of God and the fellowship of the Holy Spirit be with you all" (2 Corinthians 13:14).

The love of the Father was manifest when He sent His Son to die for us, and the grace of Jesus Christ was shown on the cross in saving us from sin and death. The Holy Spirit is the divine person who is now with us, with whom we can speak and enjoy intimate fellowship with.

It is one thing to have fellowship with the Holy Spirit, but another to enjoy His intimacy. To have fellowship with someone means to spend time with that person, talking and listening to each other. You can have fellowship with Him while you are in your car, at your job or standing in a line at the bank. You can speak with Him continually throughout the entire day.

However, to be intimate implies being alone with Him in a place where nothing and no one will interrupt you. There He will manifest Himself and show you what He has for you. That is how most of His plans for your life are revealed and you are transformed by His power. That is the place where His mysteries are revealed to you. These things cannot be learned from another human being. He wants to reveal to you all that has been freely given to you, namely the depth of His being. You do not learn this simply by reading, but by spending time in His presence.

What the Holy Spirit first reveals to you during that time of intimacy are the things that the Father has for your life. He tells you what and when to ask for things, because He knows exactly what you are going through. Then He teaches you His attributes as Provider, Savior and Healer. Finally, He shows you the deep things that are in His heart: how He thinks and what things please and displease Him. Those are the deep things of God.

When you do not seek those times of intimacy with the Spirit, you lose many blessings, but even worse, you never get acquainted with God's heart and nature. Therefore, to truly know the Father you need to have fellowship with His Spirit. He searches both God's heart and ours to make them one.

Just slip your hands up to the Lord right there wherever you are, and close your eyes. Seek Him. To be at the Master's feet with an out-of-tune, five-stringed guitar, or with a worship CD playing in the background, is the most marvelous thing in life. No matter if it's on a moldy cot or on a fine bed, in a small house or in a large mansion, with a billfold full of money or just a few cents in your pocket, always at the feet of Jesus is where you long to be. Forget your financial difficulties or the appointments you have for today. Seek Him with all your heart right now. Nothing is worth more than that priceless moment in the presence of God.

Just pray this prayer with me: "Father, please help me. I want to know You. I will not complain about being alone. I long to know You in that intimate place. I want to worship You, Lord."

Chapter 4

Behind Closed Doors

Throughout my life I have had several intimate experiences with the Lord and each one of them has left an indelible mark on my life. Even today, as I recall them, my heart is touched because they were such transforming and challenging moments for me.

The first of these happened when I was nine or ten years old, when I saw Him for the very first time. He was standing in front of my bed, suspended in the air, and even though I could not see His face I knew that He was looking straight at me. I do not remember hearing anything, except that He was standing right there in front of me. I woke my mother up so she could see Him, but she couldn't. Even though the moment was brief and I did not hear a single word, I knew from that moment on that He was watching me closely, as if He wanted to say: "I have plans for your life. I'm always going to be with you." With His presence He was telling me: "No matter what happens, you must know that I do exist and that I am the reason for your life."

I could mention many other things on these pages, but many are almost impossible to describe. I cannot find the words to explain what I saw. Every time I remember them I cannot help but weep again. It was amazing that I could see something that people beside me couldn't. It was an overwhelming thought similar to what happened to the apostle Paul on the road to Damascus.

I never forgot that moment. His appearance in my bedroom marked my whole life. I was the strange boy in class that would weep in church every time the choir would sing. I would lower my head so that no one would see me, because all my friends at school did not understand what I was feeling. I was always the boy who stopped by his friends' home at seven in the morning to go to mass. Ever since that encounter I've wanted to serve the Lord, except that in prayer I'd be asking God to make me a missionary, because I also wanted to get married. That first encounter with the Lord established the foundations of my life. I knew I was a marked man.

I Was Formed in Secret

The Word of God says in Psalm 139:13-15: "For you created my innermost being; you knit me together in my mother's womb. I praise you because I am fearfully and wonderfully made; your works are wonderful, I know that full well. My frame was not hidden from you when I was made in the secret place, when I was woven together in the depths of the earth."

In order for God to form every part of your being, He hides you and works on you in secret. The formation of our being is a perfect and masterful work; that's why the Lord did not allow a woman's womb to be transparent, so that no one could see its greatest achievement. That is why He hides the gestation process and does not make it known, not even to the parents, until the work is complete.

Even though the formation of a human being is a work of art, the process isn't really a pretty one. If we were to witness the procedure we would probably be quick to criticize or judge. We would get nervous just worrying about whether each body part is taking shape properly, or whether all of the body's organs are complete. Not to mention all kinds of suggestions we would be giving our Creator in the process, including details about family traits and characteristics. You may think that I am exaggerating, but I'm really not. Remember how difficult or challenging it was just to decide on what name to give your children? Everyone had an opinion and a suggestion. Overall I think that hiding the gestation period was the best decision, otherwise we probably would not allow it to take its course.

God has created you in a very unique way. You are one of a kind. People are not ugly or pretty, but unique. Look at yourself; there is no one else like you. Even twins have something that differentiates them. Finger-prints are an example — no two are alike. The next time you look at yourself in the mirror, recognize and appreciate the unique work that is reflected in what you see. Besides, in God's eyes we are all perfectly made; that is why we can safely say, "How awesome are your works, Lord."

> *God has created you in a very unique way. You are one of a kind. People are not ugly or pretty, but unique.*

This would be a good time to meditate on a teaching that can completely change your life. Much of what we are has to do with how we were conceived.

During the Second World War many children were born out of wedlock. Men and women from North America traveled to Europe as part of the Allied armies and had romantic relationships that bore fruit. Thousands of women conceived children outside of marriage and, as a consequence, many children were born without a father. Those who remained alone in the States lived in similar conditions. This was the beginning of a generation of orphaned and disoriented young people who, as they grew, rebelled against their parents and their own lives. Society was facing a serious identity gap. There were a growing number of broken homes, people living together out of marriage, and increased drug abuse.

You may be asking yourself why include this part of history in a book about the Holy Spirit? But you should also ask yourself what would happen if the power of God, able to raise the dead, should rest upon a person whose heart still bears the wounds of the past and has not forgotten how or by whom he was conceived? The Lord longs to give you a healthy heart, rather than wandering around from place to place with the power of God, yet still bearing the wounds of your past. He wants to anoint and transform you, but He also wants to heal you and make you whole. It is time to meditate on this and to understand that God loves you and gave His Son for you, regardless of where you came from, how you were raised or how you were brought into this world. God has a future for your life.

Perhaps you're the child of a single mother, or the product of an unwanted pregnancy whose arrival resulted in a forced marriage. Perhaps you are the fruit of a woman who was raped. Maybe you've never known one of your parents or you know that one of your parents has another family. Whatever the case may be, you might be questioning the reason for your life or even complaining that you never asked to be born. All this can easily impede your potential and limit your achievements, but let me clarify here that the circumstances surrounding your birth are irrelevant; what is important is for you to understand that God gave you this life because you are valuable and priceless to Him. That is why He put His hand inside your mother's womb and with great care and gentleness formed you, regardless of how, when or where you were conceived.

From this day forward, stop complaining. Appreciate your life, because you are unique. You cannot do anything about your past, but you can do a whole lot about your future. You were born on this earth because God has wonderful plans for you.

A Spiritual Womb

There is also a type of spiritual womb for those who are born of the spirit. When the Lord encourages us to pray, He tells us to go into our prayer closet and close the door, because He wants to shape us in secret. That garden of prayer is like our mother's womb, a place where the Lord works on us. He discovers our hearts and reveals to us what changes He wants to make.

One day the Lord asked me: "Do you know why I ask you to close the door when you pray?" That same question may be running around in many people's heads, and the answer is simple. He wants to form you in solitude. He wants to speak to you about all the good things that you are doing and how you can improve and maximize your potential. Do not be quick to accept suggestions or advice from anyone else, because it is a private matter between the Creator and His creation, between a Father and His son whom He wants to correct without embarrassing him, just as we do with our children.

He wants to form you in solitude. He wants to speak to you about all the good things that you are doing and how you can improve and maximize your potential.

In the book of Revelation, when He speaks to each of the churches, He praises them for what they're doing well and then He reprimands them, saying, "Yet I hold this against you: you have forsaken your first love. Remember the height from which you have fallen! Repent and do the things you did at first" (2:4-5). This is similar to what happens when He calls you into the secret place with Him. In a very gentle way He shapes you and corrects you, without failing to acknowledge the great traits that you have within you.

I remember one occasion when I called one of my children to come to my room in order to correct him and I left the door open. My other son walked up to see how I was going to punish him. That very moment I realized that the matter wasn't any of his brother's business, but it was an issue between father and son. So I said to my other son at the door: "Son, this doesn't concern you. Please, shut the door and leave. This is just between me and your brother.

Nonetheless, when we close the door it is not always because we want to correct someone. The most beautiful things between husband and wife also happen behind closed doors. That is when we can have intimacy. And even though there is no sin implied and it's through that intimacy that our children are conceived, we can't be inviting anyone to observe the act. In that same way, the most beautiful things between God the Father and His children occur behind closed doors. Remember, every time God calls you to that secret place with Him, it is not necessarily to reprimand us, but rather to form us and love us.

Group prayer is very good, but it is not a substitute for individual and intimate prayer, because that is the time God designed for us to have communion with Him as a loving Father. His teaching on prayer shows us that we should close the door behind us and prepare ourselves to speak with Him face to face. It is similar to many situations within marriage. When you are talking with your wife, you do not allow your children to interrupt. You ask them to leave you alone in order *You settle matters behind closed doors and allow the Lord to transform your heart.* to work things out and resolve matters with her. You settle matters behind closed doors and allow the Lord to transform your heart.

My wife Sonia and I have been married for many years and our relationship is magnificent. We mutually respect our personal space and time alone with God. Even though we often pray together, each of us also has our own prayer time because we know that our communication with the Lord is intimate and personal as well. The times that I have seen her most broken have been when she was praying alone with her heavenly Father.

God's first option will never be to send you to a prophet for reproof and correction before others. Even when correcting someone in the church, the last choice recommended by the apostle Paul was public reproof. Do not be afraid of being shaped by God. He loves you and knows the perfect way to mold your life.

Transformation Follows Confrontation

The most important revelations of my life have occurred during that intimate time of prayer. It is there that I have received the Word that has produced the results many people see today in my ministry. Much of that Word began with a confrontation. That was where the Lord questioned why my faith was incapable of buying a good pair of shoes without getting overly worried about my finances. If I could not believe for something as simple as a material thing, then I'd have even less faith to see something much greater, such as His glory.

When I asked Him to lead me towards the operation of miracles, I said, "Lord, if I had been alive during Your ministry on the earth and had seen Your miracles, it would be easier to believe in them." Then, there in secret, He softly answered, "Carlos, if you had lived during those times you would have been lost, because your manners are way too good to follow a man who spits on others."

His answer stunned me and I meditated on it for a long time. I had to recognize that on occasion Jesus did do things like spit on the ground and make mud to put on the eyes of a blind man or spit in the eyes of another or put saliva on the mouth of a deaf and dumb person. If I had not run away scandalized, I have no doubt that my mother would have asked me to please not associate myself with a carpenter who spat on people. My good manners would have competed with my faith, as it did in this instance, but the Holy Spirit was there to correct me in my secret place of prayer.

In that secret place He also taught me that I should wane my own presence in order to see His. It was precisely in those moments of solitude, in that secret place, that God transformed my life in order to make His precious anointing rest upon me. That is how I understood that prior to the anointing, we many times experience confrontation.

Psalm 51:6 tells us: "Surely you desire truth in the inner parts; you teach me wisdom in the inmost place." He has an intimate relationship with those who fear and respect Him. It is true that in a multitude of counselors there is wisdom, but how can we go to them if we do not first seek God in secret so that He can help us understand His wisdom? It is only before the Lord that you learn wisdom.

It is only before the Lord that you learn wisdom.

On another occasion I was in the living room of my house worshiping Him and seeking His will for the church that I pastor, when all of a sudden I saw His silhouette before me and I felt His presence. He spoke to me and ordered me to buy the land on which we built our first church building. Then He immediately disappeared. How I would have loved Him to stay just one more moment so that I could explain to Him that I did not have money and that He was asking me to do the impossible! But even though I did not understand, I told Him that I would obey. This was a challenge that personally changed me and took our ministry to another level.

I also remember that it was in a secret and intimate place that the Lord asked me the following question: "How much are you willing to sacrifice for Me to show My glory in the nations?" I answered: "Whatever it takes." I immediately started to look for the best way to ask Sonia, my wife, if we could sell our new house. It had taken us eleven years of savings, sacrifices and much delayed gratification to build it. When I married Sonia I had promised her that if she were patient I would build her a house debt-free. But now I was proposing that we sell the house in order to invest in the first *Nights of Glory Healing Crusade* in another country. I remember one night working up the courage to ask. Her answer took me completely by surprise: "If we are doing it so more people can be blessed, go ahead and sell it." That is how we began our international miracle meetings held in stadiums and coliseums. It was then that the Lord revealed to me that He uses those who are willing to pay the price, because they are the ones whose character is most like His own.

The television ministry started off in a similar way. I knew that the Holy Spirit wanted to speak to me about this, but I avoided the subject with Him for personal reasons. The truth is that I never wanted to be on television. I am not one of those people that like to stand out everywhere. I am also much more timid than appearances might suggest. I knew that going on television would make me a very public person, which also has its inconveniences that, due to our love for God and for His people, we have now learned to live with. At the time I was unwilling to do television and so I did not want to bring up the subject with Him, though I knew He would sooner or later. Believe it or not, I even stopped praying for a while, trying to avoid the voice of the Holy Spirit.

Suddenly something happened. I received an invitation to preach in the city of Laredo, Texas, in the United States. It was not a large meeting, in fact rather small, and the Lord led me to accept the invitation. We made all the preparations for the trip with my wife, but the flight that we took left us in another city. A co-worker from the church that had invited us came to pick us up and drove us to the city of Laredo. I was feeling very tired, and my wife ever so kindly let me ride in the front seat so that I could rest a bit. Then our driver turned on the car stereo and played some instrumental music in the background to help me rest. To my surprise the hymn *Fishers of Men* began to play, a song that I remembered singing as a little child. The words go more or less like this: "Lord, You have looked me in the eyes. Smiling You have called my name. On the shore I have left my boat. Together with You, I will seek another sea."

At that moment I began to weep like a baby and His voice said to me: "Carlos, I want you to go on television." I raised my hands and told Him that it was alright with me. Immediately He answered: "See, all I need is just a few seconds to convince you." Sobbing, I responded: "That's right, Lord! That is why I did not want to take the subject up with You." Perhaps all these things seem impossible or strange, but the results of what I am sharing here are all too visible and proven before many.

We are shaped in secret, during our moments of intimacy with God, when He shares with those who seek Him with a pure and sincere heart. He reveals Himself to those who desire Him. Do not give up;

press in before His throne. Perhaps you may never see Him physically or hear His audible voice, but I am certain that He will speak to your spirit and I have no doubt that you will be transformed by it.

The Power of Transformation

Psalm 51:7-11 continues to feed us: "Cleanse me with hyssop, and I will be clean; wash me, and I will be whiter than snow. Let me hear joy and gladness; let the bones you have crushed rejoice. Hide your face from my sins and blot out all my iniquity. Create in me a pure heart, O God, and renew a steadfast spirit within me. Do not cast me from your presence or take your Holy Spirit from me."

The writer speaks first of intimacy and the secret place before pleading for a transformation. David understood the balance, because he was already bearing the burden of his sin when he asked the Lord to change his life and let him hear joy and gladness again. God did not confront him to condemn him, but to deliver him. He does the same with you. He exhorts you and He sheds light on your sins to deliver you from them. But David did not condemn himself. He asked the Lord to turn His face away from his sins, but at the same time without taking away the blessing of His Holy Spirit because without it he would be lost.

In Psalm 51, verses 12 and 13, he goes on: "Restore to me the joy of your salvation and grant me a willing spirit to sustain me. Then I will teach transgressors your ways, so that sinners will turn back to you."

These verses speak of being used to bring people back to God. The man who refuses to enter into the presence of God so that he can be molded, corrected, and transformed can never be used to transform others. The one who seeks to achieve that balance that was in David's heart is the one who can speak into others so they can correct their lives, because his own has already been corrected and aligned.

The man who refuses to enter into the presence of God so that he can be molded, corrected, and transformed can never be used to transform others.

If you desire this in your heart, just repeat this prayer out loud with me: "Lord, change my heart. Give me a humble spirit like Yours. Give me a new heart and an upright spirit. Come and renew me so that I can help others come to know You."

Your family's transformation starts with your own life. Someone wisely said once that no one could speak to people about God without first having spoken to God about the people. We should enter the throne room of grace so that God may transform and renew us. We should go forward into His presence and say to Him: "Lord, You know my thoughts. You know that I am an immature man, that I complain; I'm self-righteous and seek excuses for everything. Change me please and transform me."

How can it be that born-again Christians who are old enough to know how they should act, many times behave in such an immature and capricious way. There are some who seek positions of leadership and cry like babies when they do not gain recognition. This type of behavior must change. Only God and His holy presence can achieve this. If you come before Him to behold His glory, He will certainly deal with you on this matter with so much love and care that it will even seem kind when He has a hard word for you.

Let me just say that everything you are feeling inside is nothing more than a thirst for God. Your soul is thirsty for the living God, not for some religious liturgy, or a certain kind of worship service, or a study of theology. What you're really feeling is an intense thirst for God Himself. Draw near to Him and drink all that you desire.

The best *Nights of Glory* are experienced before Him, the living God. Do not be dependent on a large event featuring a famous worship group or worship leader. Do not wait to be invited to a prayer vigil. Seek to experience your own private moments before the Lord. Always remember that the key to a public life is your private one. If you want success in public, first seek it privately before God. If you can choose any place to be known, let it be before His throne of grace.

If you want success in public, first seek it privately before God. If you can choose any place to be known, let it be before His throne of grace.

As we said earlier, when you close your bedroom door it is for marital intimacy. That is not a sin. But the reason you should close the door is because something intimate is about to take place. You know that it will be a time of deep gazing into the eyes of your lover, of soft and tender expressions of love, with softly spoken words.

Marriage counselors assure us that the happiness of couples who experience this type of shared intimacy reflect that satisfaction in public. The same thing happens with God and a life of prayer in the secret place. Whenever He asks you to close the door, it is because spiritually glorious moments are about to take place. You will contemplate the beauty of His holiness, you will hear the call He has for your life, and you will receive a precise vision of what God wants you to fulfill for Him. Your heart will be broken. Your whole being will be filled with joy. His anointing will rest upon you. You will hear His sweet but firm voice and, most importantly, you will leave that secret place more in love and committed to Him than ever before. So why wait any longer? Just set this reading aside for a moment and seek to be alone with Him right now. I assure you that you'll never be the same again.

Chapter 5

Wherever You Are

The Lord can manifest Himself at any time and in any place. These moments happen more commonly in church settings, when He allows us to administer His power. But there are also moments when He wants to overflow without asking our permission. Because He is an independent person who goes with us everywhere we go, and because He so desires, He can manifest Himself whenever He desires and without any advance notice.

I was once in an international airport changing from one plane to another. I never travel alone, but that particular trip to South America was the exception, and I did so because the Holy Spirit asked me to. He evidently wanted to show me the genuineness of His fellowship with me. While waiting for the flight I looked for a nice spot for a cup of coffee and a good book. Then a person walked up to me and asked if I was Cash Luna. He proceeded to ask me to please explain to him what was happening to the people. I did not understand what he was talking about, so he told me that there had been a large uproar in the immigration area because some people there had started falling to the ground filled with the Holy Spirit. Amid all the confusion, someone mentioned that I had just passed by that place and they went out looking for me. The only explanation I could give him was that, as he could see, I was in the bookstore quietly reading a book and that it surely must have been the Lord who was manifesting Himself out there among the people. While I was there, seated in the waiting area of the airport, a woman began bringing people one by one so that I could pray for them. I spent more than an hour praying for people there.

On other occasions, there have been people who I have greeted on the street who later commented that when I came near them they felt as if they were going to fall down. Things like that happen all the time, even when I am not very conscious of them. The presence of God is not limited to church buildings or religious meetings. It is real everywhere and He is able to do anything He wishes, anywhere and with anyone he chooses.

The presence of God is not limited to church buildings or religious meetings. It is real everywhere and He is able to do anything He wishes, anywhere and with anyone he chooses.

This reminds me of similar experiences of people who were staying in the hotels where Kathryn Kuhlman, the healing evangelist, happened to be staying. While she was there, even waiters and cooks would fall to the ground, touched by the Lord in the kitchen. The same things happened with Jesus. Some lepers were healed when they passed Him on the road, because the power of God touched them there. They are like those who get healed on the bus ride to a *Nights of Glory* event. While I am in the secret place of prayer, they're receiving healing by the power of the Holy Spirit who reaches them wherever they may be at. The Holy Spirit does not wait for someone to tell Him what to do. Many times, He only tells us what He did after it has already happened.

While we were celebrating a *Nights of Glory Crusade* in a city in Ecuador, something very powerful happened to a man who was wrapped in a blue blanket. He was very well known in the city because he was considered to be crazy. During the two meetings we held in that city, he never stopped teetering from side to side and drooling continually. It broke my heart to see him in such a sad condition, standing there in front of everyone without any evidence of his condition improving. The following night the scene was the same throughout the entire meeting. He continued to stand, teetering back and forth and drooling. Something inside my heart was telling me that this man could be healed. When the event was over I returned to the room they had prepared for me to use for prayer. Suddenly some people who helped us in the meetings were knocking at my door. They were very emotional and the expressions on their faces were as if they had seen a ghost. I immediately asked what had happened. They told me that while they were putting the chairs away and cleaning up the venue before closing for the night, the man seemed to react. He stopped drooling and began speaking. His first words were: "I-I-I'm-m-m-m he-e-e-a-a-a-led!" He had recovered from his insanity! No one prayed or laid hands on him; it was simply the presence of the Lord that was lingering in that area even after everyone had left, and he was healed.

His Omnipotence Follows His Omnipresence

From childhood we were taught that God is everywhere. Taking that belief to heart has a profound influence on our behavior and holiness. The Lord is always with us, regardless of where we are at or what we are doing. When you are fully convinced of this truth, you will have the certainty that He can manifest Himself wherever you are at, be it at work or in your bedroom, wherever you are studying or living, in the country or in the city, in the gym or at the church.

To long for the anointing of the Holy Spirit is to desire the manifestation of God's omnipotence in our lives. Psalm 91:1 is a prophetic word for those who seek to develop an intimate relationship with the Lord, for it says: "He who dwells in the shelter of the Most High will rest in the shadow of the Almighty."

To understand this passage we must lend special attention to the verbs "dwell" and "rest," that show us our need for the presence of God. The promise of our Lord is: "Whoever dwells in God's presence and lives with Me, sooner or later will experience the manifestation of My power in his life." The key to seeing His omnipotence is to believe in His omnipresence.

Psalm 91:2 continues, saying: "I will say of the Lord: 'He is my refuge and my fortress, my God, in whom I trust.' " Together with the first verse we see that this passage compares the Lord to three important resources that provide protection for the believer: "Shelter, refuge and fortress." A fortress is a place of defense and resupply during a time of war, a place where our strength is renewed. Our dwelling place is the place in which we experience intimate moments with the person who is closest to us. It is a personal space in which we can rest, dream and keep our secrets. The shelter protects the body from rowdy weather and other outside risks. All of this is what His presence represents for us. The anointing not only enables us to do miracles, but also provides us with divine protection. For this reason, the Psalm ends with a promise that He will deliver us from the snare and from the deadly pestilence, and that we should not fear the arrows by day, or the terrors by night, for He will send His angels to keep our feet from stumbling on any stone.

Many people seek the power of the Lord, but do not want to learn to live in His presence. They seek healing more than the Healer, prosperity more than the One who enables them to prosper, and the anointing more than the One that anoints them. They seek omnipotence while forgetting *Those who learn to dwell in the omnipresence of God will have the honor of seeing His omnipotence.* His omnipresence, because they want His power but they neither respect nor honor His existence. Those who learn to dwell in the omnipresence of God will have the honor of seeing His omnipotence.

The Foundation for Holiness

Some time ago, a person who was a habitual drinker challenged me by saying that drinking liquor was not wrong. So I asked him to pray and thank God every time he took a drink. Now just imagine this man's prayer for a moment: "Father, thank you for this drink that You have provided for me and bless this whisky so that it may nourish my body." Do you know what happened? He stopped drinking! A few days later he told me that he took the drink in his hands and when he prayed he felt the conviction of God upon him to the point that he was unable to take another drink. He discovered that God was there, together with him, and decided that he would not do what he knew would be displeasing to Him.

Believing that God is present everywhere and that He sees everything we do is a key foundation for a life of holiness. Your walk is straighter when you are convinced that you cannot do anything behind God's back. He is your companion and He is always there at your side, seeing everything that you do, listening to your every conversation and discerning your most intimate thoughts. You may be able to hide your sin from man, but you can't hide it from God.

Many years ago, when we had just opened the church, we hired a worker who stole from us. One Friday night, while I was asleep, I could see her face and at that moment God revealed to me that money was missing from the church, and that our employee was the person responsible for it. He even showed me the exact amount that she had taken. The following day I verified every detail that the Lord had showed me and I had to fire her immediately. How did I know? Because when she stole, she made sure that no one else could see her, but she forgot that God was there. I have had similar experiences on other occasions. I always remind my team that God is present in the midst of our ministry. That is a real benefit to us, because we are the witnesses of His work, yet at the same time it can hurt us if we forget that He is the one responsible for revealing the wrong things that He sees. Living a life convinced of His omnipresence is what sustains our walk with Him.

Young people must understand that it is not their parents who trouble them in their moments of passion and temptation when they are alone with their sweetheart. God is the one who makes them feel uncomfortable, because He is there at their side. It is not from the pastor that they should hide a cigarette or a beer, or before whom they should be ashamed of that liquor-filled breath. Rather they should be more concerned with their Heavenly Father's disapproval, since He is always with them. When our holiness is evident in our behavior, it is for the Lord's pleasure rather than for the benefit of any church or spiritual leader.

The problem with an extramarital relationship is not that the lovers have to be careful so that no one sees them entering a secret place together. The issue is remembering that the Lord will see them because He goes with them wherever they are. The problem is not in conducting shady business deals in secret, but rather the thought that we cannot hide them from God. It is easier to be holy when we are convinced of His omnipresence. To believe this means that when we sit down to watch television, we will avoid inappropriate scenes because we know that He is there with us watching the same program. We can trick our boss by arriving late to work, but not the Lord.

It is easier to be holy when we are convinced of His omnipresence.

It is harder to abstain from those things that please our flesh, but sadden our spirit, when we have not learned to live in accordance with the omnipresence of God. We try to justify ourselves saying that there is nothing bad in seeking our personal satisfaction, but we forget that it does not please God. It is vital that you learn to change your conduct in such matters. Your flesh will always like the things that are unpleasing to your spirit. You may not be able to remove the fleshly desire, but you can eliminate the habit. Learn to live within the shadow of God, respecting His presence at all times.

When you walk in the fear of God, your behavior reflects it because you give priority to His principles and not your pleasures. Do not try to have fun with anything that offends the One who gave His life for you at the cross of Calvary. Do not mock His sacrifice; ask Him for the strength and the character necessary to deny yourself everything that may induce you to sin. We should maintain correct behavior both inside and outside the church, since we are the dwelling place of the Almighty.

Once I was driving my car along a major boulevard in the city of Guatemala when I saw someone at the side of the road with the classic hitchhiker's thumb, so I stopped and gave him a ride. Immediately he took out a pack of cigarettes and offered me one: "Would you like a smoke?" "No, thank you. I don't smoke," I answered. "It's Friday. Want to get a beer?" he insisted. "No thanks. I don't drink liquor." "Why not?" he asked, looking me straight in the eye. By his expression, I knew that he expected a religious response. "Because my Father doesn't like it," I answered with no further explanation.

My answer puzzled him at first and he did not say anything else. In fact, what I had said seemed right and proper, so the religious question was settled.

Behaving and acting properly is not a matter of religion. It has nothing to do with belonging to a religion or attending a certain church. It is simply a matter of seeking to please our Heavenly Father. Like it or not, behavior is a matter of respecting the omnipresence of God in order to walk under the shadow of His omnipotence. We should behave on earth as if we were already in heaven, because He is in both places at the same time. Some people believe they will be close to God only after they arrive in heaven. That kind of thinking greatly limits the presence of the Lord in their lives. They leave God in last place instead of enjoying fellowship with Him right now.

Surrounded by His Presence

Someone once asked me how long I had been aware of God's omnipresence in my life. I believe that many of us were taught from childhood that God is present everywhere and that He sees everything and knows all. In fact, this is a foundational truth for those of us who say we believe in Him. On a personal basis, I have been conscious of this since I was a child, even before turning to the Lord. As a result, whenever I sinned, it made me feel ashamed to know that He could see everything. If we could be more conscious of this truth in our lives, we would conduct ourselves more properly all the time.

Let us remember what Psalm 139 says: "You hem me in — behind and before; you have laid your hand upon me" (v. 5). And then it adds: "Where can I go from your Spirit? Where can I flee from your presence? If I rise on the wings of the dawn, if I settle on the far side of the sea, even there your hand will guide me" (vs. 7-8).

Apparently, the psalmist was going through a difficult stage in his life. Perhaps he was trying to flee from God's presence. Adam did the same thing after his disobedience. The same thing may happen to us when we sin; we try to hide from God. There is no reason to abandon everything because of sin. We cannot hide from God, because He knows what we are feeling and going through all the time. He sees us in every situation. We are mistaken if we think that we can distance ourselves from God by leaving the church or getting away from Christians. His presence is not limited to the church. He is also in every place that we sin. He is with you now. When you feel sad or convicted for having sinned you can pray to Him, and He is ready to forgive you and continue the father-son relationship.

The Lord loves you so much that He dares to surround you even though He knows you are weak and make mistakes. In order to walk under the shadow of His omnipotence you must learn to behave in accordance with the omniscience of the Lord. In other words, to walk under His shadow you must be convinced that He is with you in every place and that He knows what you are thinking and doing at all times.

To walk under His shadow you must be convinced that He is with you in every place and that He knows what you are thinking and doing at all times.

Wholeheartedly believing in His omnipresence will convince you that you can hear what He is saying to you. No one gains the ability to hear Him without first adopting the right attitude to achieve it. There are people who feel abandoned when they do not hear Him, but God sometimes may keep silent for love's sake. The problem is with wanting the Lord to speak to us when we say so. God speaks when He chooses to do so. It is not necessary for you to hear Him in order to be totally convinced that He is at your side.

I am not trying to frighten you by reminding you that God sees you all the time. On the contrary, I want you to feel loved and confident because He will never leave you. Some may say: "God sees me and controls everything I do to punish me if I sin." But it is better to be grateful and think: "If He sees me all the time, it is also true that He is with me all the time and will never leave me, nor abandon me." Give Him thanks for not leaving you alone and for giving you the opportunity to walk in fellowship with the Spirit. Many people complain about their loneliness without taking into account their fellowship with God. The presence of God is real. Do not be offending Him, but honor Him with your behavior. Never say that no one understands you, because when you express yourself that way, you disregard the Holy Spirit who is always with you. Though you might feel that others have abandoned you, God will never ever do so.

Those who want to live with the manifestation of His power and enter into a new dimension of miracles, beyond their imagination, must act in faith with the omnipresence of God. Seek to experience communion and intimacy with Him. The deepest desire of my heart is that God might pour out His anointing over every area of your life!

Chapter 6

Deep Calls Unto Deep

Two friends presided over one of the largest missions' organization in my native country of Guatemala. I had always dreamt of ministering there one day because it had been the site of a powerful and well-known revival in the 1960s. Signs and wonders had taken place there continually. Even to this day, people still talk of the angelic visitation during that outpouring. Imagine what it meant for me to minister in that place and to witness a new outpouring of the Holy Spirit.

Finally the day came and I was invited to hold some *Nights of Glory* at their home church. On the first night I preached on Isaiah 61:3: "[The Spirit of the Lord has sent me] to *comfort* all who mourn [...] in Zion [...] to bestow on them a *crown* of beauty instead of ashes, the *oil of gladness* instead of mourning, and a *garment of praise* instead of a spirit of despair." I emphasized the fact that Jesus came giving the command of changing our anguish into joy and mourning into gladness.

When I finished preaching everything seemed normal. In fact, it seemed the opposite of what usually happens in other places where I minister. Nothing extraordinary or supernatural had occurred. Then I asked myself whether God was with me that night or not, and whether it was His will that I be there.

For a moment it crossed my mind that perhaps the desire to minister in that memorable place was only a personal one and not from God. As I finished my message, I told the congregation that my work of sharing the Word was done, but that the outpouring of the Holy Spirit was the Lord's business and that I hoped to see them there the following night. Suddenly, a woman seated on the fourth or fifth row stood up and began to jump and shout: "There is joy here, there is joy here." It was impossible to stop her; she was filled with laughter as she approached the altar. Imagine the scene: The church packed with people, in deep silence, all expecting to be dismissed, and all of a sudden a woman standing there half-crazy at the altar. I was just standing there in the pulpit, watching everything and praying under my breath: "Holy Spirit pour Yourself out with all Your power."

As if that were not enough, all the pastors of the church were sitting behind me watching the disorder. In the midst of the situation, the pastor in charge of the meeting asked for the microphone. That moment I said to myself: "Well, that's as far as *Nights of Glory* will go here; get ready to be thrown out."

Then the pastor said exactly what I was longing to hear: "Surely the Holy Spirit is here tonight." My first reaction was to think that this man was even crazier than me, because the woman would not stop jumping, shouting, and laughing whole-heartedly. The pastor went on: "This woman has been truly filled with the presence of God because just a few days ago her husband was killed and today this Scripture has been fulfilled in her life. Being a widow, the Spirit of God changed her mourning into gladness and her anguish into joy."

At that moment I looked toward the balcony and prayed for those who were there. They all began to be filled with the Holy Spirit and fell to the floor under the power of the anointing. Some people even experienced skin burns from the fire of God that fell down that week. Please do not ask me to explain this. The only thing that I can say is that I was a witness to all these events. We saw so many things that I could write a book just about the experiences that we shared during those days at that church. It was truly impressive and amazing, something I will never forget.

The anointing is and will always be for the purpose God sent it, for what the Word commands and not for what each of us imagines or desires.

The anointing is and will always be for the purpose God sent it, for what the Word commands and not for what each of us imagines or desires.

There are people who appeal to the anointing for everything. They have a utilitarian idea of it and think that it's a fix for everything. We need to be very careful about this kind of mindset and not play around or joke about it. Remember that the anointing is like an insignia that identifies those who have sought the Lord and His presence. Behind that search there are close, intimate encounters between God and these men and women. Respect those who have the anointing and demonstrate it publicly, because with them it is a reality and not just a concept.

More Outpouring of His Anointing

Those glorious meetings culminated with a special women's event. That Saturday, at a hotel in the city, we enjoyed a deep time of worship and praise. The moment was quickly approaching to minister the Word and the anointing, and although I knew the message that I was to preach, my faith was telling me that something uniquely powerful would happen in that place.

When the moment came to minister the word, I asked the Spirit to guide me. I opened my Bible as usual and started to share the Word of God. A few minutes later, the atmosphere totally changed and the presence of God began to descend. It was like a mantle starting to cover everyone there.

When the anointing is covering someone's life, the atmosphere of a place can change and become a place of power, not necessarily of emotion, but certainly of power.

When the anointing is covering someone's life, the atmosphere of a place can change and become a place of power, not necessarily of emotion, but certainly of power.

Curiously, some women began to be filled with the wine of the Spirit and they seemed almost drunk right there in their seats. I asked them to bring me each one of the people that was being filled with the Spirit and it turned out that they were the wives of pastors and ministers who had accompanied them to the meeting. I was so touched to see how the Holy Spirit ordered the entire meeting. Each one of the ministers and pastors was also saturated with the anointing of God, which brought an intense revival to their lives and ministries.

Once again, the anointing had surprised me. The outpouring of His power was so strong that when the meeting was over I stepped down from the platform and looked for a place to be alone with God so that I could just bow before Him and worship Him. I was completely amazed and felt a reverent fear within myself. In other words, I was afraid, you could almost even say awestricken. The manifestation of His power was so overwhelming and I sincerely considered myself unworthy of such a presence.

Thursday of the following week we went out for dinner with the pastor of that church and two minister friends to a restaurant located in the so-called "live zone" of Guatemala City, a neighborhood with a large number of eateries where people can spend a pleasant time with friends. We all asked the customary question: "Where shall we eat?" and we all gave the usual answer: "Wherever." No one wanted to make the call and we all kept saying the same thing: "You choose," "Whatever you want," "It's all the same to me."

After going around in circles we chose an Italian restaurant. When we got there it was impossible to find a table because the place was so full, so we waited a few minutes until they could find a table for us towards the side, almost in the street. The table was located in an area that anyone entering or leaving the restaurant could see. It was a seemingly normal evening. We were all engulfed in the conversation, and of course the main subject was the anointing of the Holy Spirit and His miracles.

One of the pastors was telling us about some of the wonderful things that had happened among the people at his church during that week. Then another pastor and Peruvian friend of mine, who months earlier had invited me to minister at his church, asked if I remembered a disabled man whom we had prayed for with my wife. Of course I remembered him, because on several occasions he had been filled with the Holy Spirit sitting there in his wheelchair, although I did not understand why he had not been able to walk. My friend told me that he later received a phone call from Peru and the caller shared that when the man arrived at church the following Sunday he walked in without a wheelchair and without the help of his sister, who had always assisted him. Finally, during that evening of fellowship we shared many similar testimonies that left us all simply amazed.

These miracles should have made me feel very good because I was the one who had ministered on many of these occasions and I could feel the power of God with me. Of course, there is no one called by the Lord to the ministry who does not desire to be used by Him. Anyone in similar circumstances would feel very happy, but that was not my experience at that moment. I soon began to feel empty, even more so than before receiving His anointing, although the feeling was entirely different.

I began to sob like a child going through a difficult moment without his parents to help him. I wept with a sensation of loss, the way someone at a funeral mourns the loss of a loved one. What I did not know was that I was weeping over my own funeral.

This was happening to me right there in plain sight, in front of the whole world, sitting in that place with crowds of people walking by me. Naturally, everyone started looking at me. Even my friends were puzzled by what was happening to me and even to this day, they do not understand the extent of it, because I never fully told them what I was experiencing. It was overpowering, that feeling of death inside of me, and, well, that was exactly what was happening. I was filled with a deep desire to die to myself. I wanted to be an automaton for God, a robot completely obedient to His every command. I didn't want to have a will of my own anymore.

Of course, that is not what He wants for us; on the contrary, He wants us to serve Him voluntarily and to live to obey Him. Please, do not misinterpret my words, but the only thing I desired at that moment was to not live for myself one more minute. I longed to live totally for Him, only for Him, and not for the ministry which I led, not for anything or anyone else. I have always asked the Spirit of God: "Not I, but you, Lord. Not my presence, but Yours." But this time the feeling was so overwhelming that this simple prayer expressed the greatest desire of my life.

Although some people may think that I am mistaken, the only thing that my heart deeply desired was to live like a robot, without questioning or doubting even the simplest of His commands. I wanted to be a complete slave of Jesus and His precious Spirit, though I am a son and an heir of His.

The only request inside me was: "More of You and less of me, Lord." I asked the Holy Spirit what was happening to me and why I felt emptier than ever before. At that moment He brought to my mind Psalm 42:7, which says: "Deep calls unto deep in the roar of your waterfalls; all your waves and breakers have swept over me." There I found the answer to what I was experiencing. Deep was calling to deep so that I might be placed directly under His cascading power and filled with Him.

On the night that my wife and I sank into the bed during the visitation of His presence, that deep "desire for His anointing" was filled. For eleven years I had prayed asking for at least one drop of His anointing to quench my thirst. When His power came upon us, this deep "desire for His anointing" had been filled and it called us to another deep thing, which was the "desire to be used with power." At the moment that this second deep thing was filled, I was immediately called to a third deep desire, which was the "desire to be completely obedient to God, to be fully yielding to His will."

Then I understood that in that restaurant I was yearning to obey Him in everything. I was longing to go wherever He might lead me and not where I wanted to go. I longed to say only what he would command. I was eager to apply that same level of obedience in every area of my life, my family and my ministry. I repeated again and again: "Deep calls unto deep in the roar of Your waterfalls."

When one of your deep things overflows with the Spirit, go and find within yourself another deep area that is empty, and call for it to be placed under that same cascade to be filled. For example, if you feel an inner emptiness in your life that was filled by the presence of God and then after a period of time you once again feel an inner emptiness, this is probably not the same one, but rather another deep thing in a different area. It is possibly a deep area that "desires to love God in the

As long as you drink more of Him there will always be another deep area to be filled under His cascades.

same way that He loves us." When that depth is filled, it calls out to the deep area of "holiness" that it also may be filled by the cascades of the Spirit. As long as you drink more of Him there will always be another deep area to be filled under His cascades.

The Deep in Your Being

What deep area is being discovered in your being at this moment? Go and present it before the living God, because He will fill you. When we spend time in the presence of God, thirsty for His love, He fills us and He does so in His way and not as some people might imagine. Many people think that God will give them a glass filled with water, but they are mistaken; He gives us to drink just as He does for a small and thirsty gazelle that comes panting to the bank of a river to quench its thirst.

The psalmist tells us: "As the deer pants for streams of water, so my soul pants for you, O God. My soul thirsts for God, for the living God. When can I go and meet with Him?" (Psalm 42:1-2).

The deer when thirsty does not seek a glass of water, but rather approaches the river's flowing currents to drink and quench its thirst. The deer appears at the water's edge just as you and I should present ourselves before the Lord. If you are thirsty for Him and want to drink of His presence, if you want to drink the wine of the Holy Spirit, you should answer the same question that the psalmist asks himself: "Where can I go to meet with God? When can I spend enough time before Him to satisfy my thirst? When?"

It is not a matter of seeking water to fill a glass. You must go and immerse yourself in His river. The deer approaches the flowing waters and begins to drink and drink, and soon realizes that "all your waves and breakers have swept over him." He is no longer on the shore, he is not just trying to get a little water at the edge of the river; he is now completely immersed within the current.

That is how God is with those that genuinely thirst and seek for Him. He does not give them water to drink from a cup or a jar, nor does He restrict them to the edge of the river. When He sees you drinking of His presence, He takes you and completely submerges you. Then without realizing it, all His waves and breakers are sweeping over you and you find yourself totally immersed in Him, drinking continually.

Spiritual thirst is different from natural thirst that is physically experienced by our bodies. Our natural thirst is satisfied when we drink water; but spiritual thirst increases when we drink of the Lord. The same comparison can be made with physical hunger that disappears when you eat. In contrast, spiritual hunger only increases with each serving taken from the Word of God. My prayer is that one day, after so much eating and drinking from His Word, you will become solely dependent on His presence and His Word.

Chapter 7

What Strange Orders!

The first time I prayed for the healing of a person, something rather unexpected happened. Sonia and I were still dating and while I was walking her home one day, I received a message on my pager. That same night there would be an all-night prayer meeting at the church that I was attending and someone from there was trying to reach me to say that my presence was needed at the church.

When I arrived, the person who was scheduled to preach greeted me and told me that he would not be able to minister, and that the preacher that night would be me. Surprised, I asked him: "Why?" His answer was: "You're up in ten minutes, get ready." At that moment I thought of the typical excuse: "Could you not have let me known fifteen days ahead of time so that I could prepare myself and do God's work better?" If I had given him that kind of answer, what I would really be doing is defending my own ego. People often do that to avoid risks. But God loves to use people who have died to their own desires. So instead I asked the Lord what I should preach about and He responded: "Talk about healing and about faith."

Instantly I obeyed. After I finished preaching about faith, one of the elders of the church approached me and said: "I have one leg longer than the other, could you pray for me so that the shorter one will grow." I had not even touched the legs of the man and every eye in that venue was already on me to see what would happen. Imagine the pressure I felt at that moment! What if nothing happened? What if, instead of the shorter leg growing, the longer one shrank? What would everyone say if the leg did not grow?

If you are honest with yourself, you will realize that in such moments of pressure your thought is not going to be: "What do these people think of God?" but rather: "What will everyone think of me if nothing happens?" No one likes that kind of pressure and that is why many do not dare to minister the anointing. That night I took the leap of faith and held that man's leg in my hands, closed my eyes and said aloud: "Father make this leg grow."

When I heard the shouts of people around us, I immediately opened my eyes. That very moment the leg started to grow there in front of all those around me. It was a miracle visible to everyone. It was glorious! Right away, everyone wanted me to pray for them, and soon there was a long line of people waiting for their miracle. That night we saw a large number of healings.

The Holy Spirit is a gift that God has given to us, not an award. Of course, walking in the power and the anointing of the Holy Spirit depends on us and our obedience. At that prayer meeting we witnessed great miracles because of my obedience when told that I would be the one to minister. I did not resist or complain because they had just asked me a few minutes before the meeting.

The Word of God says in Acts 5:32: "We are witnesses of these things, and so is the Holy Spirit, whom God has given to those who obey him." And in Psalm 45:7 we read: "You love righteousness and hate wickedness; therefore God, your God, has set you above your companions by anointing you with the oil of joy."

The presence of the Holy Spirit is a gift God gave us so that we might know that He is always with us and will never leave us alone. We only need to ask and He will give it to us. Now then, the anointing is different. It is the power of God that covers a person and follows him wherever he goes. The anointing comes upon us through obedience that we give to the Lord by believing Him. It is He who wants to anoint you and give you power, but to receive it you must be obedient to His commands and instructions.

The anointing comes upon us through obedience that we give to the Lord by believing Him.

Untying the Donkey

Many times God asks us to do unusual things. Even though for us it may seem impossible, He does it to shape and mold us. We can see this in His Word, for example, in the story found in Luke 19:29-34.

On that occasion, the Lord sent two of His disciples to a neighboring village, telling them that they would find a donkey tied up that no one had ever sat on. He ordered them to untie it and to bring it to Him. He also told them that if the owner were to ask what they were doing, they should simply respond by saying that the Lord had need of it.

105

Imagine for a moment the command that was given to these disciples and their reaction when they heard it. It would be similar to your boss sending you to a neighboring city to take a new car from a dealer, and telling you that you are simply to say: "It is for my boss." I can just picture the two disciples chatting with each other, going over how strange this command was that the Lord had given them. Perhaps their conversation might have gone something like this: "Do you realize what the Master told us to do?" "Yeah," the other one answered. "The owner's going to think we're trying to steal his donkey, and he's going to come after us." "Don't you think it would be easier if we just chip in and buy a new donkey for the Lord?" When they arrived at their destination and found the donkey tied up, they probably said: "Who is going to untie it?" "Not me!" "Okay I will loosen it, but if they ask anything, you answer."

In spite of all the questions and doubts they might have had about that very unusual instruction, they obeyed Jesus' command.

In those times when God asks us to do something that is unusual or difficult for our flesh, that is when we must die to our own egos and pride. It is during those times that God shapes us so that He can anoint us.

In those times when God asks us to do something that is unusual or difficult for our flesh, that is when we must die to our own egos and pride.

We as human beings have a problem when we talk about the anointing and the issue is usually around the vessel God chooses to transfer it or the person whom God has anointed, because most people find it hard to walk in obedience. We want to obey a God that we cannot see, but it is difficult for us to obey the people that we do. Therefore, God shapes you by setting authorities over your life that give you orders and correct you.

As a child, in everything you do, you are subject to someone else: your parents at home, your teachers at school, or your boss at work. God does this because He wants to give you His power, but He knows that there is nothing more dangerous than a person who is anointed yet disobedient. That is why the Lord has you submit to authorities. He wants you to work on yourself and die to your own flesh.

Obedience is what makes us die to ourselves. Creativity, desires and aspirations that we might have will not help us in this process. The obedience that we demonstrate toward the Lord helps us die to our own flesh, ego and pride. It helps us embrace the decisions that the Holy Spirit leads us to.

By giving them these unusual instructions, the Lord Jesus was shaping His disciples to walk under the anointing that He had in store for them. He was training and teaching them to obey the One whom they could see, so that later they would obey the One they could not. Once they learned to obey, it was Jesus himself who would give them the Holy Spirit to guide them.

Personally, I believe that at the time there must have been other people who were more prepared than the disciples whom Jesus called. However, these were the ones who showed a greater willingness to serve and follow Him. There were surely people who had much better strength of character than Peter. He was impulsive, always armed and even once cut off someone's ear. Some pastors would not have even had him directing traffic at their churches! John and James wanted to set fire to a whole city, in Samaria, because they were not well received there, and they even dared to make that suggestion to the Lord. In spite of all their defects, however, they were obedient and that was the tipping point with Jesus.

When we walk in obedience to Him, His power is manifested in our lives. If you want to walk under the anointing and if you want the power of God to be manifest in your life, you must be obedient to the commands and requests that the Lord has given you. You must also obey the orders that you receive from earthly authorities such as your parents, professors, pastors, bosses and others, obviously though when and if these do not imply some kind of sin.

> *When we walk in obedience to Him, His power is manifested in our lives.*

Tax Payment

We find a similar story in Matthew 17:24-27 concerning the payment of the temple tax. Some tax collectors challenged Peter, asking him whether his master paid his taxes just like everyone else did. Beyond their interest in the money, they wanted to find some fault in which they could accuse the Lord.

When Peter returned home he did not tell Jesus anything about it. It was Jesus who brought up the subject and said that, although they should not be subject to taxes, in order not to offend them, He would pay them. Then He told Peter to go out to the sea to fish, but He gave him specific instructions to cast his hook in the water and said the first fish that he caught would have a gold coin in its mouth. With that coin, Peter should pay the taxes for both of them.

Just think about this for a moment. Peter was a professional fisherman who cast his nets into the sea to make a living, and he even had other employees under him. He was a businessman, a man who fished with nets, not with a fishing pole. Imagine how Peter might have felt about having a carpenter tell him how he was to fish. That might have seemed offensive, reason enough for a fisherman of Peter's expertise to ignore such an instruction. But that was not all. In addition to telling Peter to fish with a fishing rod, Jesus also told him that the first fish he caught would have a coin in its mouth with which to pay the tax. What fish carries a coin in its mouth and then bites a hook? Anyone who knows anything about fishing would see what an absurd idea that was, but Peter did not stop to think about it; he simply obeyed.

I can just imagine what the tax collectors were thinking. At that moment they might have seen Peter leaving with a fishing pole on his shoulder, heading towards the seashore.

"What a strange sight!" they might have thought. Peter might have sat down by the shore and thrown his hook into the sea, not knowing exactly what to expect. He turned around looking from one side to the other, hoping that no one else would be watching him, and then he spotted those surprised tax collectors who would not take their eyes off him. These were the same men who had accused him of not paying his taxes, and now they were watching him with his fishing pole there by the sea. The great fisherman now seemed like an amateur. I dare to say that they might have even mocked him, insinuating that he was refusing to pay the tax, and questioning how he expected to get a coin from fishing. They could have said: "You left the nets to follow a man who does not pay his taxes and now all you've got is a fishing pole." In spite of all the humiliation that he may have experienced, Peter did not drop the fishing rod until a fish bit the hook. He pulled it out of the water curious to see what kind of fish this was that had swallowed a coin and how he would find it. To the surprise of those who mocked him, the coin was right there in the first fish, just as Jesus had told him.

Going fishing that way might have seemed humiliating to him, but this is the only way that we can die to ourselves. Peter had learned that when he obeyed, the hand of God was upon him and everything would turn out well. Do not forget that Jesus also experienced humiliation on the cross of Calvary, and therefore after He was resurrected, He said that all power had been given to Him. The anointing rests more powerfully on those who are required to do things they do not like, things that cause them to die, yet they do not turn away from doing them. These are the ones who do not give excuses to defend their lives, their egos or their reputations to avoid doing what they have been commanded to. On the contrary, they have set aside their pride and have refused to hide behind any type of appearance of spirituality that might impede them from walking in the anointing of the Holy Spirit. For that reason the Lord goes with them, everywhere, with His power.

The anointing rests more powerfully on those who are required to do things they do not like.

The Man with a Pitcher of Water

The third example I want to give you is found in Luke
22:7-13. The day had arrived for the Jewish Passover
and the Lord would celebrate this occasion with His
disciples. He asked Peter and John to get everything
ready. He told them that once they entered the city they
would find a man carrying a pitcher of water. They
should follow him to see what house he would enter
and then they should ask the owner of the house for
the upper room where the Lord would be eating the
Passover with His disciples. They did this and after following the man with the pitcher of water, they entered
the house and prepared the upper room for the Passover.

I imagine that Peter and John had not really thought
about what Jesus had asked of them until they started
on their assignment. In those days men did not carry
pitchers of water; that was a woman's job. It seems
that they never thought about how strange it would
be to find a man carrying a pitcher of water and even
less about how it might look for two men following him throughout the entire city until he entered a
house. That man with the pitcher must have walked
strangely and everyone in the neighborhood would
have known him, but the surprise was that this time
he was not alone, but was being followed by another
two men. I think that some people might have started
chiding or mocking them, others may have whistled
and said things to them. Though they were dying
to themselves, yet they did not hesitate to obey His
instructions.

Just think for a moment about the instructions that
Jesus' disciples were obeying. Imagine how difficult
it was for those men to go and untie a donkey and

have the owners questioning their reasons, or how illogical it was for Peter to go fishing in order to take a coin out of a fish's mouth when surely there were better ways than that to pay taxes. Those two apostles who had to walk around the entire city following a man who was carrying a pitcher of water probably felt humiliated or at the very least uncomfortable, but what the Lord was seeking was that they might die to their flesh and learn to obey.

Later, the Lord took those two men who went to get the donkey, brought them before the Holy Spirit, and said: "These men can't see You, but I've trained them to follow My every command, so that though in their minds it might seem ridiculous or absurd, they will obey. If they are able to go untie a new donkey and bring it to Me, they will be capable of doing whatever You ask of them."

I suppose that He also went to see Peter and said to him: "Come, I'm going to introduce you to someone you cannot see, but whom you can obey, because if you were able to obey My order to go and take a coin out of a fish's mouth, wait and see the orders that He's going to give you." And He must have taken him to the Holy Spirit and said: "He was willing to obey Me in matters that might have seemed unusual, so I'm sure he's capable of obeying You as well."

He would have also called those two who followed the man carrying the pitcher of water and probably said of them: "I know the discomfort you went through that day, but I also know that you are no longer common, ordinary men because you have learned to obey." And He must have taken them before the Holy Spirit and said of them: "I present to You these two men who were able to follow a man carrying a jug of water out of obedience. I entrust them to You because I know that You will anoint them."

Now I ask you: "Can the Lord take your hand and say to you, 'You have obeyed your parents and those in authority over you,' and then present you to the Holy Spirit? Can the Lord take you by the hand and lead you with His Holy Spirit because you have obeyed those you can see in everything, thus assuring that you will obey Him whom you cannot see?"

It's a Question of Obedience

Discipleship to our Lord Jesus is comparable to the education that a father gives to a daughter whom he will be giving away some day at the altar. He teaches her to be submissive and obedient to him so that one day he can take her in his arm and give her away to someone else. On that day he'll be able to say to the groom: "For years I have trained and educated her; I am sure that she is a submissive woman who will honor you in everything. Therefore I know that everything will go well with you."

To disciple is to form someone in order to assign him to another person. If you learn to obey those whom you can see, the Holy Spirit will be able to trust you with His powerful anointing. He knows that if a son is able to obey his parents even when he does not understand their instructions, or if a worker is able to submit himself to his boss even in the most difficult moments, then he will be capable of obeying God in all things. He places us under authority so that we can be molded and our attitudes

He places us under authority so that we can be molded and our attitudes made evident.

113

made evident. In this process the Holy Spirit keeps a close eye on us to see who will obey Him.

This is why, years later, the apostle Peter was used to take the Gospel for the first time to the Gentiles and thus open the door of salvation to all of us who are not Jews. The Spirit visited him and gave him a vision in which he saw a large sheet coming down from heaven with every kind of animal, some clean and others unclean, and he heard a voice that said to him: "Get up, Peter. Kill and eat." He resisted doing so because he had never eaten the flesh of unclean animals, but he heard the voice of the Lord saying to him: "Do not call anything impure which God has made clean." At the same time some men, sent by the Lord, visited the home where he was staying to ask him to go with them to Cornelius' home, where the Gentiles were waiting for him to speak to them about the Kingdom of God. As with all Jews, it simply didn't seem right for Peter to visit the home of strangers, much less non-Jews, but he understood the order of the Lord not to call unclean anyone whom He had sanctified.

We must get used to obeying even without fully understanding. The Apostle Peter followed the instructions that the Lord had given him and he went with them. Even though going to such a place perhaps wasn't to his liking, he did so without hesitation. He went to the Gentiles because he had been shaped on the day he went fishing and got a coin out of the fish's mouth. He was one of those who obeyed the strange order to walk around the city following a man carrying a pitcher of water. It is for that reason that when the Holy Spirit needed a man to take the Good News to the Gentiles, He knew that He could count on Peter. The anointing was poured out for the first time on them because God found in Peter, an obedient man.

There are people who desire to have the anointing, but they do not want to maintain a relationship with the Holy Spirit that gives them the anointing. Generally speaking, people pay attention to the gifts that the Holy Spirit can give us and they want to have them, but they do not follow His instructions or let Him guide them in their daily living. When you believe in God, you obey His Word. No one can say that he believes in God if he does not obey His Word, because what is truly believed is reflected in the obedience demonstrated towards it.

I believe that the miracles of the Lord are manifested in my life not only because I have a special gift, but also because I have obeyed His order to pray for the sick. Praying for the sick is a command that we all have received, not only those with a healing ministry. Dare to lay your hands upon the sick and believe that miracles will happen. Do not fear the stares of those who would criticize you if nothing happens to those you pray for. The anointing follows your obedience. As long as you are not willing to obey and do what you do not like to do, you will never see a powerful anointing in your life and ministry. You may have moments of anointing and you may have good times in His presence, but to see the power of God flow on a continual basis in your life is a matter of faith and obedience.

As long as you are not willing to obey and do what you do not like to do, you will never see a powerful anointing in your life and ministry.

Chapter 8

Ministering Unto the Lord

People constantly ask me how much time I devote to prayer. They believe that the amount of time spent in prayer is proportionate to the amount of anointing that is poured out in church meetings. I never like answering that question because it does not depend on what they are thinking. The Bible does not equate the effectiveness of a prayer with the time that is spent on it. If that were true everything would be so simple because then just by "speaking like parrots," or repeating words, people could increase the anointing of God in their lives.

When people ask about prayer, they often imagine that more power is derived from the duration of a prayer than from God himself — the one who answers that prayer. What is important is to pray in faith, because "to him that believes, all things are possible." The apostle James teaches us that the effective prayer of the righteous can accomplish much. The word "effective" is connected to "efficiency" and means to achieve objectives in an appropriate timeframe. Therefore, your prayer should be efficient in order to produce the fruits and the answers that you desire.

Another question that people frequently ask me is what kind of price we need to pay to get His anointing. My answer is that the Lord Jesus Christ is the one who paid the price on the cross of Calvary by shedding His blood for us all. His sacrifice opened the door for us to receive the Holy Spirit. There is nothing I can do through my own efforts that can ever be greater than the price already paid by our Lord Jesus Christ. It would be arrogant on my part to say that it was my years of prayer or sacrifices that achieved an outpouring of His anointing.

I have heard some people say that living in holiness was the price they had to pay, but in my case all I had to do was obey the one we call "Lord." It is what we are expected to do. Others say that traveling and leaving my family to care for the work of the Lord is part of the price, but the same sacrifices are made by physicians who make house calls or military personnel who are transferred from base to base. The same thing is true of those who must get up early in the morning or stay up late at night in order to tend a sickbed. Isn't this the same thing that pediatricians are required to do when helping sick children? Do other people in the workplace not also get exhausted working in their professions when they want to achieve their goals? Why then do Christian leaders think that we are the only ones called to "pay the price"? We simply cannot place a price on the anointing that anyone could pay. Jesus Christ has already paid the entire price and it is faith in His completed work that allows us to see His glory.

To pray and seek His face is not a price to pay but a delight to enjoy. It is the greatest pleasure of all. How can you label being in the presence of God and wor-

To pray and seek His face is not a price to pay, but a delight to enjoy.

120

shiping Him as a sacrifice? I seek Him because I love Him, not because it is a requirement for the anointing. I pray and ask Him for things because He is my Father and I trust in the One who wants to give me all things. I diligently seek Him, continually, even when I am tired, because I love Him.

Useful and Obedient

In the book of Luke 17:7-10 we read a great teaching the Lord gave us regarding the work and service that we owe to those in authority over us: "Suppose one of you had a servant plowing or looking after the sheep. Would he say to that servant when he comes in from the field, 'Come along now and sit down to eat'? Would he not rather say, 'Prepare my supper, gird yourself and wait on me while I eat and drink and after that you may eat and drink'? Would he thank the servant because he did what he was told? So you also, when you have done everything you were told to do, should say, 'We are unworthy servants; we have only done our duty.'"

In this passage the Lord presents us with a new perspective on serving. I want to show you three important things in this story that will transform your performance at work and your search for the Lord. The first of these concerns obedience, the second concerns respect, and the last is about girding yourself to minister unto the Lord.

Obedience at work is a requirement that you are expected to fulfill. Many prefer to do what "comes naturally" or "what they feel like doing" rather than what is asked of them, showing that behind their "creativity" and "ingenuity" lies a resistance to authority. If you want to grow at your workplace, promptly do what is asked of you. This does not mean that it is wrong to

121

make your opinions known. It simply means that your first priority should be to diligently fulfill whatever you are asked to do. Those in authority will promote people whom they can trust. So obedience makes you someone qualified to receive a blessing.

Do not expect others to always be thanking you for what you do and do not be frustrated when you do not receive any recognition. On the contrary, always be grateful for what you receive, even when no one thanks you for what you are doing. In this passage the servant sees himself as "unworthy," even when he was obedient in everything. All he did was what he was told to do. He did not expect the gratitude of his boss because he knew that a servant does what he is ordered. This may seem harsh, but it is not the Department of Labor who wrote this. According to the Word of God, when we only do what we are told, we are "useless" workers. We only start being useful when we do beyond what is expected of us.

Jesus taught obedience to His disciples. He prepared them to be obedient even when they could no longer see Him. This way they would learn to follow the leading of the Holy Spirit whom they could not see. We must teach our children obedience, so that they will remember and put into practice your values when you are no longer with them.

Remember that an obedient person is one who is able to do as he is told, and a useful person is one who does more than what is asked of him.

Remember that an obedient person is one who is able to do as he is told, and a useful person is one who does more than what is asked of him. The useful servant is the one who does more than what is asked of him. Jesus is looking for people who are useful and obedient.

Respectful and Ready to Serve

Many years ago, it was considered customary to honor leaders and the elderly in our communities. It was considered proper to take a gift to the schoolteacher or to give him an apple. Now anyone who does that sort of thing is labeled a "teacher's pet." It was also common to see students respectfully standing to their feet in unison to greet a guest in the classroom. Nowadays, they do not even turn around to look.

The daily tasks of the servant in the parable were to till the ground and to shepherd the flock. But he was also asked to do other things that could not be ignored. He had to return to the house after an arduous day of work and tend to his master. Nowadays few people want to do more than what is required of them. It's probably this lack of commitment that has brought us to the current financial crisis and the present-day lack of values and moral decline.

Today it is difficult to find a secretary who is attentive and detailed and who genuinely serves her boss without hidden interests. I thank God that I have an efficient assistant who still stops to ask whether she can leave even when it is past her work schedule. I can also ask her to make me a cup of coffee even though this task is not listed in her employment contract as one of her duties. This is the right attitude to have. You should be the worker who passes by the boss's office to offer him a glass of water and ask if anything else is needed. Show yourself as a servant who does not hold anything back. Look after your boss and go over and beyond the tasks that are assigned to you, just as you minister unto the Lord and not only to the work He has called you to do.

Prepare Yourself to Receive a Blessing

In the parable we read that at the end of the day the master does not ask the servant if he is tired. He simply asks him to prepare his supper and then gird himself and serve him. Later, after the meal, only then is the servant allowed to eat his portion. This is a great promise. If the servant had retired at the end of the workday to his house with the other servants he would have eaten the meal prepared for the daily workers. But by going into the master's house, preparing his supper and serving him, he had the opportunity to eat the same food as the master and, best of all, spend time in his company at his table. The servant who obeys and tends to his master receives better food and a greater blessing at the end of the day. This implies an extra effort, because it requires him to do something that was not normally his responsibility. The key is to gird yourself because girding yourself implies subjection.

In order to exert a greater effort we should gird ourselves in preparation for service, because there will always be a reward for those who do so.

Those who must lift heavy weights, such as weightlifters or furniture movers, utilize a belt or girdle that serves as support for the abdomen and protects their vertebrae. That is precisely what we should do. In order to exert a greater effort we should gird ourselves in preparation for service, because there will always be a reward for those who do so.

The fresh Word of God and the revelation God blesses me with do not come from tending the flock but rather from girding myself when I have no more strength left and ministering unto my Lord. I lift my hands and say to Him: "Here I am, ready to serve and minister unto You. Tell me what else you desire."

At the end of the day, present yourself before the Lord, serve Him His meal and ask Him what else you can do for Him. You can be sure that His answer will be: "Stay here, eat with Me and we will talk."

Always offer the best meal unto the Lord because you will surely partake of the same food. Give Him the best worship because He will honor you in the same way. Set aside a special time for worshiping the Lord and ministering unto Him as you have never done before. Gird yourself and tend to your Lord's desires.

Do not be a useless servant. If you are tired, find a belt to support you. Draw your strength from wherever you can and always give more than what is asked of you. Tend to the one who gives the orders, without regard for what others may say or think. Being a good child of God requires that you be a worker who is diligent and outstanding. It does not matter what your particular job is. Always show commitment and be useful. And most importantly, tend to your Lord; never lie down to sleep without first serving Him His meal and sharing a time of fellowship with Him.

The Danger of Personal Concerns

We all know the story of Martha and Mary, two sisters who invited Jesus to dine at their home. While Martha was preoccupied with her household duties,

Mary was sitting at the Master's feet, listening to Him. Martha was upset with her because she was not helping and she asked the Lord to reprove her, but He responded that only one thing is necessary and that Mary had chosen the best part.

Martha was very concerned that everything be in proper order for her guest. She was productive, but she did not give herself time to listen to the Lord. There is nothing wrong with hosting a banquet and taking the time to make sure that everything is done with excellence, but this should not be done with the wrong attitude. God does not want us to be lazy or negligent, but neither does He want us to be overly concerned about our daily routine. He knows very well that physical stress can damage our bodies, strain our relationships with family members, and, above all, affect the intimacy of the relationship that He wants to have with each one of us.

It often takes time to learn that the most important thing in this world is your time alone with God. Mary discovered this and Jesus would not deprive her of that gift. Excessive worries about life and the deceitfulness of riches conspire to separate us from His presence. There are those who have lost that intimacy as they struggled to get a higher salary, a larger house, or a better job in the ministry. They worry so much about different things that they have not taken the time to discover what is truly valuable in life. They have not understood that man does not live by bread alone but by every Word that comes out of the mouth of God.

Take time to listen to God. If you want to hear Him, you must free yourself of everything that burdens you. Cast aside the worries and anxieties of your mind, otherwise you will not be able to hear the promise of God for your life. You must tend to the one you serve. It is not enough to work all day for the Lord. You must also spend time with the One who created you, who gave His life for you and jealously desires you.

We need to serve the Lord, but we must also take the time to hear His voice. That will keep our hearts from being filled with worries to the point of complaining to Jesus, just as Martha did on that occasion. We cannot allow our activities for the Lord to serve as a substitute for our relationship with Him.

In Quietness and Rest

The Bible teaches us in Mark 6:31 that the Lord Jesus took His disciples to the wilderness because there were so many people being ministered to that they could no longer find time to eat. Why did He take them to a solitary place? Because He wanted them to rest! Likewise we should rest every day. When we take short breaks, we lower our stress level and we no longer need extensive and expensive vacations to recover. The will of God is for us to work and also to rest, that we find our own solitary place to meditate on God. You should not be afraid of solitude because it can actually be very productive.

When the Lord wanted to free His people from slavery in Egypt, He gave specific instructions to Moses to pass on to the Hebrews. But we are told in Exodus 6:9 that "they did not listen to him because of their discouragement and cruel bondage." When they became very discouraged by

When they became very discouraged by their work, they stopped listening to the great promises God had for them.

127

their work, they stopped listening to the great promises God had for them. The same thing happens to us when we are hastily rushing around, because He is the God of rest and meditation.

How long has it been since you had contact with nature? From home to the office, from the office back home, from home to the television set, from the television set to the Internet, from the Internet to the cell phone. My mistakes are usually due to impatience provoked by an uncontrolled anxiety. We need to beware of impatient prayers! We need to set aside all the things that provoke stress and tension so that we can know God. When your head is filled with the worries of life you cannot hear God, because your mind is troubled. Free your mind so that you can focus all your attention on His promises.

We cannot truly know God in the middle of the ruckus that surrounds us in these modern times. He can manifest Himself in public, but He also likes to make Himself known face to face, in solitude. Psalm 46:10 says: "Be still, and know that I am God." The word "still" in the original Greek language, when translated into English, means "relax." This is rich advice that will help us improve our intimacy with God.

Effective Prayer

Learning to pray effectively is a process. The process of prayer is as unique to each individual as the way a father educates his children. God is our Father and He wants to teach us the basics of a good relationship with Him. We should not make a doctrine out of the form of prayer that each person uses to approach the Lord in intimacy. Prayer is so personal that we can only share our experiences. Each knows at what time and way is most convenient for him to seek intimacy with the Lord.

If you are learning to pray, it is good to establish a schedule that you can follow in order to create the habit and shape a discipline in your life that you may not have had before conversion. This is why I was very strict on myself when it came to praying from six o'clock to eight o'clock in the morning. During that time I came to realize that during the second hour I repeated much of what I had already prayed in the first hour. So I reduced the time because I understood that the quantity does not determine the quality of the prayer. It was necessary for me to pass through that stage of maturity, because all the time invested in prayer helped me to work on my faith. We feel the need to repeat things over and over again, not because we think that God does not hear us, but because in doing so we are working on our own faith. Jesus said that we should not abuse prayer with vain repetitions, but not all repetitions are vain. For example, practice and repetition help us to achieve perfection and confidence in our handwriting. Once you learn to write, you do not need to continue with penmanship exercises, because you have developed a good handwriting.

After years of being disciplined and responsible in my prayer time, the moment came when God taught me to trust in Him more. When we started the *Nights of Glory* healing crusades, my prayer schedule changed and I abandoned my discipline of praying at six in the morning. Because many of the meetings ended after midnight, it was very hard to wake up early the next day to pray. Thus I faced a great internal conflict. I did everything possible to keep that schedule, and it became more and more difficult. I even rebuked Satan because I thought he was interfering. But the anointing did not diminish; on the contrary, God's manifestations in my life were becoming more evident. I felt insecure about ministering without praying as I had before, but even so more miracles occurred and we heard more testimonies. It was then that the Lord told me that He was dealing with my faith. He wanted me to have confidence and to simply feel secure that I was doing what was necessary. Apparently I was trusting more in the amount of prayer, rather than in my continual communication with Him throughout the day.

On one occasion my small children asked me to play with them just when I was getting ready to pray. I could not set aside their demands for attention, but neither did I want to deny my Lord and I needed time alone with Him. At that moment I heard Him say to me: "Do you think I will stop anointing you because you play with your children and fulfill your responsibility as a father?" So I decided to stay with them and jumped and played, even though on the inside I continued to worry. That night I felt a great peace when I was about to minister. I was surprised to see that while I was walking toward the platform, people began falling over, touched by the Holy Spirit. Anyone might have said: "This man has been praying intensely," when the truth was that I had just come from jumping on the bed with my children. The only thing I could do was trust the voice of God who said to me: "I will be there. I am the One who does the work."

The Lord taught me to trust in Him, but not to be irresponsible with my time of prayer. The important thing is to understand that there are things learned in prayer and others that are learned by simply trusting in Him. One cannot take the place of the other.

The story about Moses trying to pray before the Red Sea summarizes my life. God said to him: "This is not the time to pray, just extend your rod." This meant that the moment was not for a time of prayer, but for action. Personally, it cost me a great deal to understand that there are moments when it is no longer time to pray, because the Lord is ready to do His work. It was very difficult to apply this truth in my life because what I had achieved until that time was the fruit of eleven years of intense prayer. It was hard for me to understand that I had moved to another level. I felt guilty and condemned myself for not praying as much as before. I faced a problem in my conscience, until I learned to develop confidence without losing my love for my time of prayer.

Now I am convinced that God will not leave me if I am not able to have my prayer time as planned. Even so, it is important to remember that confidence is no justification for negligence. Continue praying, lest by becoming overconfident you get to be like the champion who underestimates his adversary and is defeated.

The quality of prayer is discerned by the results that it produces. A man who communicates with God is identified by the ambience of wellbeing that surrounds him. There are those who make prayer an end in itself rather than a means to an end. They think that dedication to prayer will make them holy regardless of what they pray. Let us remember that in the Bible prayer has always served to accomplish something. Elijah prayed that it might not rain for three and a half years. At the beginning of your life of prayer you may ask twenty times for something small. But once your faith has grown, you will pray one time for something twenty times greater.

We learn to pray by praying. Nothing about prayer can be taught to someone who does not pray. Learn to work with yourself, spend time with the Lord contemplating Him, and not just making petitions of Him. By seeking and knowing Him in depth, your prayers will become more effective. It is very similar to when your children have gained the confidence to ask you for something because they know you and they know the right time to ask. The key is to find the appropriate time. When you ask for something at the right time, you will obtain it more easily. Communication with God is a virtuous circle: "The more time you dedicate to prayer, the more you know Him, and the more you know Him, the better your prayer."

Learn to work with yourself, spend time with the Lord contemplating Him, and not just making petitions of Him.

Chapter 9

The Natural and the Spiritual

The Holy Spirit is a teacher par excellence. He has a unique method of teaching every student, as if He were giving customized and personalized classes. He imparts His lessons as each person has need, according to the individual's characteristics. For that reason I believe that He has taught me in a unique way that He may not use with other people.

One of His lessons broke down one of the biggest barriers in my Christian walk. This occurred when He taught me from the passage in 1 Corinthians 2:9-12 that the Holy Spirit is the one who reveals to us not only the things of God and the deep things of His heart, but also the things that the Father has freely granted to us. He knows before we do what God wants to give us, and He whispers it to us so that we can ask for it in prayer, knowing that when we do so His answer will be "yes." It is like the child who, hearing that his parents have decided to give his brother a bicycle, runs and tells him so that he will ask for it.

With this teaching I decided to turn to the Holy Spirit in prayer and ask Him to show me what I should ask for, believing that He would reveal to me what the Father desired. His answer would take me completely by surprise. Until that day I had many prejudices about asking Him for material things and believing that the Lord wanted to provide for me. But He changed that in only three nights. On the first night, when His presence filled my bedroom and I asked Him what I should ask for, I heard His sweet voice telling me: "Ask for a house. He wants to give you one."

Needless to say, it was a challenge for me to ask for a house, but I obeyed. At first it surprised me that He would influence me to ask for that, because for me it was a material thing that should not be so important as to take the time to pray for it. But the Spirit insisted, and He told me that the Father had already granted it to me and that all I had to do was ask. As soon as I asked for it, my whole body was filled with the presence of the Lord. I felt as though I were swelling up due to the strong sense of His power resting upon me. In fact, years later, my wife and I were able to build our house just as we had desired, free of debt and with peace of mind.

Motivated, I returned the following day to my prayer room and the Spirit spoke to me again. This time He took me to another level. He told me to ask for an auditorium filled with young people, because God wanted to give it to me. At that time I was a youth pastor at my earlier church. I raised my hands, and while I was asking for this I had a vision of a full auditorium. The same presence that came over me on that first night returned to my room. That group of young people that I was pastoring became the largest in my country.

On the third night I returned knowing that He would take me to a higher level. This time the Spirit spoke to me and said: "Now ask for more of Me, because the Father wants to anoint you." At that moment I could feel the glory of God filling my entire room and His powerful presence resting upon me. His anointing came to rest upon my life.

In many ways asking God for something is similar to purchasing something online. You order it today, you pay for it instantly and therefore it becomes your property, but it takes a while for the distributor to send it. Ask God for something today. Believe that He has granted what you have asked of Him, and have faith that He will bring it to pass.

Ask God for something today. Believe that He has granted what you have asked of Him, and have faith that He will bring it to pass.

That is how the Lord led me from asking for the material to asking for the spiritual. But even as I was being taught this lesson, I was still unaware of all the plans that God had in store for my life and ministry.

Years later, after going through the process of seeing these three requests answered, I realized that the Lord is so complete that He provides everything that is necessary to bless people. The *Nights of Glory* are a clear example of how these three aspects work together. The Holy Spirit, in His mercy, has placed in me this beautiful gift of healing so that we can see sick people be made whole. He has given me the gift of faith to believe that the people will come and that He will provide the resources necessary to cover all of the expenses involved in blessing them. Could you imagine that someone might have all the material resources and yet not possess the gift of the Holy Spirit to bless them? Or the other way around, can you imagine having the gift of the Lord to minister healing to people, and yet not have the resources needed to even reach them? This is why it is necessary to believe God that He will give us all things.

When the Holy Spirit motivated me to ask for the material, the ministerial and the spiritual, He knew what the final outcome would be of the instructions that He was giving me. The Lord will not use us without training us beforehand and He will not do so if we are not willing for our *status quo* to be broken by His Word and His teaching.

Now I have the faith to build a larger church, one that I envisioned more than twenty years ago. I also have the determination to see it filled with the anointing, which will bless everyone who comes. We must have a holistic and balanced faith to accomplish these goals because partial faith is not sufficient for us to reach the overall objective.

If you believe that the anointing is upon you then you must realize that it is to bless someone else. The more people you want to bless, the more resources you will need. Therefore, you must have faith for the material as well as for the spiritual and God specializes in providing both.

A Faith Challenge

In our spiritual and material life we should always believe for and seek the best. In my life I have learned that faith for the material complements my faith for the spiritual. Everything that you see now in our ministry, from our growing church to the *Nights of Glory* events, has been a direct result of believing in Him.

There is nothing wrong with using your faith to prosper from day to day. This means believing that God will prosper you in everything you dedicate your time and effort to. Do not forget that one of the promises that God made to Joshua was that if he were diligent and courageous, he would prosper in everything that he undertook. Therefore, every time I embark on a new undertaking, I believe that God will prosper it. Another example of this was Joseph, son of Jacob. Even Pharaoh understood that God was with him, for everything that he did prospered.

There is nothing wrong with using your faith to prosper from day to day. This means believing that God will prosper you in everything you dedicate your time and effort to.

To believe God about prosperity, on a daily basis is like going to the gymnasium of faith and exercising your muscle of confidence. He will give you the victory on the day of the true battle. That is why there are situations that challenge our faith on a daily basis, because the Lord wants you to keep on exercising it and winning the battle. Just as an airplane flies due to the force known as lift, faith is kept alive by the challenges that often present themselves in our lives. You will not be able to fly without lift or suspension, nor will you be able to live if you have not fought the battle of faith.

We cannot speak of winning if we have not run the risk of losing. We cannot speak of overcoming, unless we have faced adversities. Even though some may want to believe that faith should not be used to prosper, I will continue to do so. I will take on the daily challenges that God brings my way, believing that He will give me all things in Christ. Just as I believe that

He can use me to heal thousands, I must also believe that I will have the necessary resources for this blessing to reach even more people.

He Did Not Spare His Own Son

In Romans 8:32, the apostle Paul asks a question: "He who did not spare his own Son, but gave him up for us all —how will he not also, along with him, graciously give us all things?" If God already gave us His Son, surely He will give us anything else that we request or may need.

Let me repeat the same question that Paul asked: If the Father gave you His beloved Son, and gave Him up to die a humiliating death on the cross of Calvary, do you not believe that He wants to give you all the material things that you need as well? Do you believe that the material things you ask for are more important or costly to the Father than His only Son? If He has already given you the life of the One who is much more valuable, He will not deny you what is material. When you receive Jesus in your heart, you must also believe that you will receive the blessings that come with Him.

If you were to voluntarily give me your son, and a little while later I ask you for food to sustain him, what would you do? Wouldn't you give it to me if you have already trusted me with your son? What father would give you his son to be wounded and crucified and then refuse to give you anything else?

The Lord wants you to exercise your faith every day and believe that everything you need and desire will be given to you.

The Lord wants you to exercise your faith every day and believe that everything you need and desire will be given to you. If you do not trust God for material things, who do you expect is going to give them to you? The God who gave you His precious Son also wants to give you everything else.

Christ was offered up for your sake. When you have a financial problem, you can say to the Lord: "I will sleep in peace, because if you have already given me Your Son, I will not lack anything else." Whenever you need something, go back to the cross and tell Him: "If You have gone so far as to give me Your Son, I know that You will also give me everything else that I need, Father." Place your faith in Christ who died on the cross and you will obtain the fullness of what the Father purchased for you in that place.

If God placed within your heart the One that has no price, He will also give you everything else that does have a price. Only Jesus has been exalted to the highest place. If the Father has already given you the highest thing in the universe, how can you think that He will not give you everything else?

When the Bible declares that God did not spare His only Son and that He will not deny us other things, in that context the Scripture refers to those things that we need to make known to the world the good news that God has given us His Son to save us. Therefore, all of us who want to take the message of our Lord Jesus to the entire world should also believe that He will provide everything else needed to achieve that objective.

This teaching about prosperity is more spiritual than many of you believe and it is only for mature people in the Lord. If the Lord gave you a body, why would He not give you the means to sustain and clothe it? The body that he gave you is much more valuable than any clothing that you can put on it. Think about it: What is the value of the skin covering your body or of one of your organs? If you had to pay to restore any part of your body, it would cost a fortune. Just imagine the value that it has! If He already gave you skin, will He not also give you clothing to cover it? If He already gave you what is most valuable, it would be illogical to think that He will not provide what you need to care for yourself. Yes, God longs to prosper you.

Ask and It Shall Be Given to You

If the Lord taught us to ask of Him, then why are there people who say it is wrong to ask? He came to teach us the truth that makes us free, and one of His teachings was to ask. Freely asking is the natural attitude of a trusting child. I ask God with the same persistence that I had as a child whenever I would ask my mother for something. I would do whatever was necessary to get her to give me what I asked for! I would climb on her when she was asleep and pry her eyelids open. Then I would put my face as close as possible to hers and say: "Mom, my bike! When are we going to get my bicycle?"

Do you believe that God does not like His children to ask Him for things? As a father I am pleased when my children ask me because it means that they trust me. It would be terrible for them to ask others and not their father. When my children turn up with things that do not belong to them, I tell them: "Take it back, that's why you've got a father here." Neither does God like you to confide in anyone else for your prosperity. Then why don't you want to ask God for everything that you need for living? And how can you ask that His glorious anointing be with you if you are not even able to ask Him for the common things of daily life? Jesus taught us to ask because He knows that the Father wants to give them to us.

Ask in confidence. Jesus said that if we ask, it would be given to us; that if we seek, we would find; and if we knock, it would be opened unto us. Look at what the Gospel of Luke says: "Which of you fathers, if your son asks for a fish, will give him a snake instead? Or if he asks for an egg, will give him a scorpion? If you then, though you are evil, know how to give good gifts to your children, how much more will your Father in heaven *give the Holy Spirit to those who ask him!*" (Luke 11:11-13; emphasis mine).

There are three things that we can learn from this verse. The first is that the Lord wants to give you His Holy Spirit. If we, as human fathers, being evil, when our children ask for food do not give them stones or serpents, how then can you think that God will not give you His Spirit when you ask of Him? If you ask God for His presence or the fullness of the Holy Spirit, He will give it to you. If you ask for the anointing, He will anoint you. Ask Him! Do not wait any longer, but pray believing. Ask Him to pour out His Spirit in abundance, and He will do so!

The second lesson is that He motivates you to be a father who gives good things to your family. This is why the fullness of the Holy Spirit is not for the stingy or greedy, but rather for individuals who know how to give. There are many men wanting to be anointed servants of God and yet they do not know how to give a warm hug or a kiss to their wives, much less a nice anniversary gift. People who walk hand in hand with the Holy Spirit know how to imitate the Father in a good way. Why would the Lord not give you the Holy Spirit if He sees that you give the best to your children and to your spouse? The Lord wants to fill with His glory those parents who desire to lift their families up.

Dear parent, the Lord wants you to be the one who asks for good things for your home. Do not forget that while you are a responsible parent who provides for your own, you are also a son, and as such, God expects you to ask Him for things.

Do not forget that while you are a responsible parent who provides for your own, you are also a son, and as such, God expects you to ask Him for things.

The third and last thing is that the Word compares the fullness of the Spirit to our daily food. It speaks to us of a balanced diet based on fish, eggs, and bread. This comparison isn't by accident. When I asked God about this, He showed me His desire to make us understand that the Spirit is indispensable, more so than food. If on average we eat three meals a day, we should be seeking His presence with the same frequency. What the Lord is saying is that you need both food and the Holy Spirit and that you should seek Him with the same energy with which you work to earn your daily sustenance.

There are people who believe that the Holy Spirit is not for everyday living. When you go home and ask what's for dinner, your wife won't say that there isn't anything because you already ate something yesterday. Yet when it comes to the Holy Spirit, there are those who say: "I was filled with the Holy Spirit at a certain retreat or conference." Every day we choose what we are going to eat, yet we relegate the Holy Spirit to certain occasions without realizing that we need to drink of Him all the time.

Just as we cannot live without eating, we should not live without the Holy Spirit. The body becomes weak without food and the spirit dies without His presence. God gave us life so that we might live abundantly, being filled with His Spirit. Every time you come to church you should walk in and go: "Today I want to be filled Lord."

The Holy Spirit and Good Things

Let us look now in the Gospel of Matthew at the same passage that we read a little earlier in Luke about asking. Notice that the Holy Spirit inspired a different Word at the end of this passage: "If you then, though you are evil, know how to give good gifts to your children, how much more will your Father in heaven *give good gifts to those who ask him?*" (Matthew 7:11; emphasis mine).

We read in Luke that the Father wants to give the *Holy Spirit* to those who ask, but now we see that Matthew says that He wants to give *good things*. When inspiring the Scriptures, the Lord made a point of saying in Matthew and in Luke that the Father is able to give us the Holy Spirit as well as good things if we ask for them. It's very important for Him that His children believe that they can ask for His presence and fullness, just as they can ask Him for good things. Both come from the Heavenly Father.

The phrase "good things" in the Greek means "something good, beneficial, useful, healthy and pleasing." It also means "pleasant, producer of joy, excellent, distinguished, honorable, and of good quality." That is to say that the Lord gives things that are useful and pleasant. That is why He says: "He will not give him a scorpion, or a stone." God gives you something for your wellbeing, but this does not necessarily mean that He will give you for your sinful pleasures. For example, you cannot ask for the Internet to see pornography. You never give your children something that will harm them. The Father not only provides, but also educates us at the same time. There are children who do not behave well and yet they want everything. Likewise, there are people who misbehave and want to have good things. That is not possible.

Faith is needed to receive both things. I must believe for both the Spirit and the things I need. I cannot say that I have faith for the Holy Spirit to anoint me, and then not ask for the things that I need to live, such as groceries, the rent, or my bills. You need faith to ask that the glory of God be with you, in the same way that you need it to ask for His daily sustenance. The faith to see miracles is the same faith that I use to pay for the healing crusades, for transportation of the equipment, the sound system and the lights. God is interested in spiritual matters as well as our material needs. We need faith to receive both. Learn to ask and receive everything that He has for us.

You need faith to ask that the glory of God be with you, in the same way that you need it to ask for His daily sustenance.

146

Chapter 10

His Dwelling Place

One night as I was praying in my room, preparing to minister for a healing crusade, the Lord gave me a Word. He told me that people would come to the *Nights of Glory* seeking a miracle for their lives, and that He could give it to them, but then the following day their bad habits would make them sick again. That was the day that God completely opened my understanding to see that I cannot be expecting divine healing without tending to my body's health as well. I cannot believe for supernatural miracles without caring responsibly for my physical body.

That night the Lord gave me a promise. He told me that He would increase the anointing upon those people who respected their bodies and gave it the importance that it deserves. It is like having your own house but paying someone else to care for it. No one likes to live in a place that is all dirty and disorganized, full of cobwebs, mildew or humidity. That is why we must take care of our bodies, so that we can offer the Holy Spirit a dwelling place worthy of His habitation. When we take care of our bodies we are saying that we value Him and that we are consciously preparing for His infilling.

The Lord revealed to me that He anoints bodies, not spirits; He anoints minds, not souls. When Jesus said: "The Spirit of God is upon me," the Spirit was like an ointment on a person. The anointing travels throughout the body, from head to toes, and is imparted by the laying on of hands. We read about it in the Bible: "It is like precious oil poured on the head, running down on the beard, running down on Aaron's beard, down on the collar of his robe" (Psalm 133:2).

There are those who believe that the body is something material, transient, of little or no importance in the spiritual world, but if that were so, why then will we be given a new body in the resurrection? Because we're even going to need one in eternity!

Some people look down on the body that God gave them and believe that taking care of it is just vanity. They think that it has nothing to do with holiness or with God and that we should only guard the mind and the spirit. But that's a mistake. Otherwise, why would the apostle Paul say: "May God himself, the God of peace, sanctify you through and through. May your whole spirit, soul and body be kept blameless at the coming of our Lord Jesus Christ" (1 Thessalonians 5:23)

Your body is the dwelling place of the Holy Spirit. The Scripture says that you should not defile the temple of God. That temple is your body. The book of 1 Corinthians chapter 3:16-17 warns us that whoever destroys the body, God will destroy them. This is a very strong warning that we should heed in order to protect ourselves, for God lives in each person's body.

A Holy and Living Sacrifice

All of us know that while on earth, the Lord had a

body. That is why He had to be born of a virgin and grow as a child. We lose sight of how vital the body was for the fulfillment of His purpose. In 1 Peter 2:24 we read: "He himself bore our sins in His body on the tree, so that we might die to sin and live for righteousness; by His wounds you have been healed."

Jesus bore our sins in His body and by His wounds we were healed. He reconciled us to God in His body, through death, to present us as a holy people. God considers the body so valuable that our redemption became a reality through the sacrifice of Christ's flesh and blood, not through His spirit or His presence.

God considers the body so valuable that our redemption became a reality through the sacrifice of Christ's flesh and blood, not through His spirit or His Presence.

Just for a moment, imagine Jesus with His disfigured countenance, a crown of thorns on His head, His back lacerated by a whip and His side pierced by a spear. Those wounds were where He bore our sicknesses and by them we were healed of cancer, arthritis, migraine, diabetes, and any other human infirmity. Imagine all the infirmities leaving the bodies of men and entering Christ's own body on the cross at Calvary. Before that time His body had been healthy and whole. In order to bless your body, He submitted His own as a curse.

As a lamb destined to be sacrificed, Jesus had to present His body perfectly. Hebrews 10:10 makes it clear: "And by that will, we have been made holy through the sacrifice of the body of Jesus Christ once for all."

151

Jesus' offering was His body, prepared by God to be sacrificed on the cross. He had to take care of it because it was to be presented free of imperfections, healthy and whole in order for it to bear all the misery of the human condition. In the same way that He had to be free of sin in order to bear our sins, He also had to be free of infirmities in order to bear our diseases. Can you imagine the blood that Jesus shed on the cross being full of cholesterol or triglycerides?

The body was very important to our Lord Jesus. Our salvation depended on it. He took care of His health because He knew that in His body He would present a sacrifice that was pleasing to the Father. The veil of the Tabernacle represented His flesh, and we were given access to Him when it was ripped open. Today, you can enter into the most Holy Place through Jesus Christ.

The apostle Paul also tells us that we should care for our bodies so as to present ourselves as a living sacrifice unto the Lord: "Therefore, I urge you, brothers and sisters, in view of God's mercy, to offer your bodies as a living sacrifice, holy and pleasing to God—this is your true and proper worship. Do not conform to the pattern of this world, but be transformed by the renewing of your mind. Then you will be able to test and approve what God's will is—his good, pleasing and perfect will" (Romans 12:1-2).

When you come before the Lord you present your body. We worship in spirit and in truth, but we do so by raising our hands unto Him, by singing and dancing before Him. For this reason, when you pray just ask yourself: "Will the Lord accept the way I am treating my body, or am I sinning by presenting an unworthy body to Him?" If we do not see God working more in our lives it is surely because there must be something we are missing. If you want more anointing in your life, you must have more respect for your body, because His power moves upon and through it. The more you sanctify yourself, the better the offering will be that you present to the Lord. Your mind will be transformed.

> *If you want more anointing in your life, you must have more respect for your body, because His power moves upon and through it.*

The one who learns how to present his body before the Lord will experience the renewal of his mind and will live happily in the good and perfect will of the Lord.

Love Him with All Your Strength

The Bible teaches us that the first commandment is: "Love the Lord your God with all your heart, with all your soul, and with all your strength" (Deuteronomy 6:5). When God speaks of strength He is referring to the strength of the body. That's another reason why we should take very good care of our bodies by feeding and nourishing them correctly. We are to love God with our heart and soul, but we also love Him with the strength of our bodies. That's why we should seek to be as healthy as possible.

The body is for the Lord and the Bible teaches us that everything that we do should be motivated by an earnest desire to please Him. God is balanced and doesn't go to the extremes. He does not call you to be careless, nor does He call you to worship the body. Caring for your body is not the same as living for it. Philippians 3:17-19 tells us: "Join together in following my example, brothers and sisters, and just as you have us as a model, keep your eyes on those who live as we do. For, as I have often told you before and now tell you again even with tears, many live as enemies of the cross of Christ. Their destiny is destruction, their god is their stomach, and their glory is in their shame. Their mind is set on earthly things."

There are two ways to make the body a false god. The first of these is to live for it, with your sole objective being to look good unto others, but not to present it to the Lord. The other is to neglect it, making it a victim of gluttony and desires. As you can see, taking care of your body has nothing to do with being fat or thin, but with respecting it as the temple of the Holy Spirit.

Take a minute and reflect on the way you treat your body. Change your habits if you are a person burdened with anxiety who uses your body for excesses. Leave behind the vices that damage it, but also those foods that end up taking a toll on your health. You should choose carefully what you eat. He has given you the responsibility to be wisely selective. God has given you an appetite and a stomach to digest food, but that does not mean that you should eat more than is necessary. Exercise self-control, work out and seek to stay healthy. Focus on using your body to glorify God above all.

Care for the Body and Service to God

Many years ago, before we had inaugurated our second church building, we used to rent a warehouse for our meetings. We got to the point when we were holding six services every Sunday. I would preach in every one of them. By the end of the day, I would feel exhausted. Often I would have a fever and find myself trembling. My spirit was willing to preach more, but my body couldn't handle it. That's when I came to realize that weariness is an enemy of the anointing. When my strength is drained, prayer becomes more difficult and it is harder to believe that God will move. I decided to

> When my strength is drained, prayer becomes more difficult and it is harder to believe that God will move.

be more careful about what I ate and to exercise more in order to have greater resistance. This would enable me to minister to more people. If I do not take care of myself, I greatly limit my ability to give to others.

I want to serve the Lord for many years, even when I am of old age. I must maintain my strength and health. In order to achieve that, I must take care of myself now while I am young. The body tends to wear out and deteriorate, so if you want to serve God more, you've got to take care of it! You will only be able to serve Him as long as your body holds out.

In order to care for my body, I try to rest, eat healthy and exercise regularly. These are the foundational pillars of good health. I have learned that the body is like a plant that grows better when a drip irrigation system is providing it with the exact nutrients necessary for healthy, wholesome growth. It is difficult to choose whether it is more important to satisfy our bodies or our cravings, because we generally eat what we like and not what we need to stay healthy. This is the reason why we often feel drained of energy and end up with physical ailments. Personally, I always try to eat a balanced diet. I do not deprive myself completely of small delights, because all that the Lord provides for us is good with moderation.

I also exercise and drink a lot of pure water. I work out and do cardiovascular exercises on a regular basis, since we live in a world that is too sedentary. We go from the bed to the breakfast table, then to the car, from there to our desks, etc. Our routine could hardly be more sedentary! We spend more time seated than standing, so our hearts are not as efficient as they should be to pump blood throughout our bodies. We obviously need to make some changes.

I also try to sleep more. Resting allows us to renew our strength and our minds, in order to have more energy during the day and a clearer mind for making decisions. Those who do not rest properly will end up exhausted and tend to get irritated very easily. In the long run, this is a serious issue for those who serve God.

An illustration of what it means to care for the body as the dwelling place of the Holy Spirit can be found in bottled water. We cannot drink without a glass or vessel. That's why we need to be sure that the glass is always ready to be filled. We cannot create the water, but we can bottle it. Because water is such a vital element, it is only logical to have a good bottle to house it in. This analogy serves to illustrate the care we must have for our bodies. If we want to be filled with His presence we must care for our bodies, which are the vessels that He fills. Surely the Lord will deposit more in a vessel that is well cared for.

The care and use of our bodies is intimately linked to our spiritual lives. For example, the disciples of the

Lord, even though they wholeheartedly desired to follow Him, were unable to pray with Him for even an hour on the night that He was arrested. That is why He said to them: "Watch and pray so that you will not fall into temptation. The spirit is willing, but the flesh is weak" (Matthew 26:41).

If you really want to increase your faith, you should pray at the best times, not when you are tired or worn out. David said that he would seek the Lord early in the morning because it was the time of the day when he was most alert. Others are accustomed to seeking Him in the evening, since that is the time of day when they have the most energy. However, there are many Christians who no longer pray because they end up leaving it for last, after all their chores are done and they have run out of strength. The absence of bodily strength hinders us from seeking the Lord, even though we desire it with all our hearts. That is why you should manage your time and strength to better seek Him intimately. Fasting is another spiritual practice that is related to how we treat our bodies. It brings many benefits, including the exercise of self-control. If you can abstain from food to which you have a right, you will also be able to abstain from other things that are forbidden. The exercise of self-control is what makes fasting a powerful tool for increasing your faith.

You should manage your time and strength to better seek Him intimately.

If you think about it, our life of faith is directly proportional to the way we treat our bodies and it is more important than we have ever thought or believed.

Someone Else's Property

Your body belongs to God because you were purchased through Jesus Christ. Therefore, it is only logical and natural that God lays claim to your body, because it belongs to Him. You have no grounds for doing as you please with it. After the Lord, only your spouse can put demands on your body.

In 1 Corinthians 3:16-17 we are warned: "Don't you know that you yourselves are God's temple and that God's Spirit dwells in your midst? If anyone destroys God's temple, God will destroy that person; for God's temple is sacred, and you together are that temple."

The word "sacred" or "holy" in the Bible means "set apart." Your body is holy because it is the temple of the Holy Spirit. That is to say, it is set apart first for God and then for your spouse. That is why the scriptures say, "Food for the stomach and the stomach for food, and God will destroy them both. The body, however, is not meant for sexual immorality but for the Lord, and the Lord for the body" (1 Corinthians 6:13).

Think of how many things are always competing for our bodies! Why do you think one of the strongest influences in television is pornography? It persuades us to use our bodies in the wrong way. By doing so the Bible says that God Himself will destroy us, because we are destroying His temple. The devil's strategy is to lead you toward the destruction of your own body and force God to fulfill His Word by destroying you.

The Reason I Take Care of Myself

I have seen many young people who start dieting and working out at the gym prior to getting married because they want to look good for their future spouse on their honeymoon. This is good, but it would be much better if they did so first for the Lord. It is also good to take care of yourself to avoid getting sick, but the presence of God and His love should motivate you even more. Can a honeymoon or the danger of death due to an ailment, be more important than the fact that your body is the temple of the Holy Spirit? There are many things that may motivate you to take better care of your body, but the correct one is to realize that it is the dwelling place of our God and Creator.

The Holy Spirit lives in your body. When you dress yourself, ask Him if what you are putting on seems good to Him. You cannot say that Jesus is your Lord if you do not even allow Him to run His own home — your body. If you truly say that your body belongs to God, show it! Those of us who are called to the ministry have the responsibility to take good care of ourselves so that we can answer to our Lord and reach the prize that He has given to us.

You cannot say that Jesus is your Lord if you do not even allow Him to run His own home — your body.

One day, something is going to motivate you to take care of your body. It may be cancer, high blood pressure, your honeymoon, a tournament, a sport, or it may be Jesus. Will you take better care of your body because you have been diagnosed with cancer? Will you eat healthier because you have high levels of cholesterol? Will you exercise more to avoid heart failure? Or will you keep your body in good, tip-top shape to present it unto the Lord as a living sacrifice that is holy, acceptable, and pleasing unto Him?

It is not a matter of religion to care for and respect the body simply because it is the temple of God. It is the vessel that we present to Him spiritually as well as the vehicle for His anointing. When you touch your body, you are touching part of Christ. For this reason, we could safely say that the way you treat your body is really the way you are treating Christ.

Chapter 11

Used by Him

One evening while I was in fellowship with the Spirit of God, the Lord began to speak to me about a key element for the continued growth of our ministry. I was meditating in bed, as I often do, and He spoke to me and told me that there were three areas of resistance that we should learn to manage.

The first of these, He told me, was that Satan is our adversary. He reminded me of the Scripture that says: "Submit yourselves, then, to God. Resist the devil, and he will flee from you" (James 4:7). He showed me how we must learn to resist his attacks, so that when he realizes that we are not going to give in, he will flee. This is a type of resistance that's widely known among the people of God, and it's the easiest to understand and accept.

Then the Lord showed me the second area of resistance and He took me to the passage in Acts 7:51 where we read: "You stiff-necked people, with uncircumcised hearts and ears! You are just like your fathers: You always resist the Holy Spirit!"

Here He taught me that people resist the Holy Spirit because their hearts are hardened. They oppose the work of the Lord. It would seem more like a generational issue, since there have always been people that have opposed the apostles and prophets of God who have operated in signs and wonders and spoken in His name. He told me that I should resist evil, but not to resist His Spirit, which is good. When we stop resisting the Holy Spirit and the work that He wants to do in our lives, we'll begin to walk in fellowship with Him.

The third area of resistance is the one that most often receives the least amount of attention and that concerns the offenses committed against us by others. I understand how these factors stop us in our tracks from becoming the men and women that God wants us to be. If anger, bitterness and resentment are allowed to provoke us and build a nest in our hearts, they will hinder the beautiful flow of God's grace in our lives.

The Lord was clearly saying to me: "This is the area of resistance in which many of my children and ministers have fallen. I am unable to take them to another level because of this." He also added: "To those preachers who do not know how to handle offenses I only speak to them to reveal a Word for My people, but I will not have intimacy with them." I understood that bad feelings we may harbor against someone directly affect our relationship with the Holy Spirit. It disturbs our fellowship with Him. God can use you, but you won't have the best relationship with Him that you would otherwise enjoy.

I understood that bad feelings we may harbor against someone, directly affect our relationship with the Holy Spirit.

How can God use someone who has lost fellowship with Him? Remember Jesus said one day people would come to Him saying that in His name they cast out demons or healed the sick, and that He would answer them: "I never knew you, depart from Me." They were used for miracles, but they did not do His will; they were supported, but not approved. If God blesses someone, this does not necessarily mean that the person's life or works received God's approval. God is like the father who supports his daughter on her wedding day even though he does not approve of the way she made her decision. This is why you cannot hide behind the flow of the anointing, but you must seek for God's approval in the secret place. This is the main reason why we need to overcome this resistance.

Free of Offenses

We must forgive every offense against us, intentional or not, for if we do not forgive God will not forgive our own sins. The day that we choose not to forgive a sin or an offense that someone has committed against us, we stunt our growth because God will stop answering our prayers.

On that transforming night the Lord said to me: "There are sins people commit against you that I am going to take charge of, but there are others that are only offenses, and those you need to handle."

There is a difference between sins and offenses. Not everything that offends us is a sin, and we should have the maturity to accept that not every sin committed against us should offend us. Many people sinned against the Lord Jesus, but He was never offended or embittered. Instead, He forgave them. On the other hand, even though Jesus never sinned, there were people who were offended by Him. Do you remember when He declared that He was the bread of life and that whoever ate His flesh would never be hungry again? Many felt offended and stopped following Him.

Unfortunately, some people have not forgiven others for things that God does not even consider sinful. Think of how many workers are resentful towards their bosses because they were corrected for arriving late? How many children are offended with their parents after being corrected? We cannot judge something as sin only because it offends or grieves us.

God will deal personally with people who have sinned against us, but at the same time He expects us to deal with the offenses that have been committed against us so that these things will not hinder the blessings that He wants to pour over our lives. When you feel offended, do not fall prey to making yourself the victim. Do not try to justify a lack of forgiveness, but rather live free of offenses and learn how to overcome every painful thing that others may have done to you. If you want the Holy Spirit to use you in a mighty way, you must be a person whose heart, mind and soul are healthy and free of all bitterness.

If you want the Holy Spirit to use you in a mighty way, you must be a person whose heart, mind and soul are healthy and free of all bitterness.

The Lord dealt forcefully with me in this area, not so that I would learn to resist the devil, for I had done that all my life as a child of God. He did not do so to keep me from resisting the Holy Spirit, because He knows that I love Him and that I let Him do whatever He desires in my life. He wanted me to be careful with this third area of resistance.

We are all subject to the criticism of others and we run the risk of allowing wounds to remain in our hearts. In my case, as a leader, I have inevitably become a public person without seeking it. I am sometimes called to account because not everyone agrees with what I teach and believe. Others have risen up to lie and criticize me without knowing the truth. They have made things up about me even as I, in turn, demonstrate an attitude of blessing towards them. If I am not careful, this situation can easily cause an internal conflict in me. The Lord was clear when He told me that I should not give in to the offense. He wanted to use me in a powerful way. He wanted to lift me up even higher and my anger should not be a wall stopping the flow of His blessings. An attitude of forgiveness can only be achieved if the heart remains clean and free of offenses.

The Guardian of My Soul

Read 1 Peter 2:20-24: "But how is it to your credit if you receive a beating for doing wrong and endure it? But if you suffer for doing good and you endure it, this is commendable before God. To this you were called, because Christ suffered for you, leaving you an example for you to follow in his steps. 'He committed no sin, and no deceit was found in his mouth.' When they hurled their insults at him, he did not retaliate; when he suffered, he made no threats. Instead, he entrusted himself to him who judges justly. He himself bore our sins in his body on the tree, so that we might die to sins and live for righteousness; by his stripes you have been healed."

This passage begins with a reference about learning to suffer for doing what is good and standing up to injustices done to us with a good conscience in order to be approved by God. Immediately following this he tells us that the Lord is our example of the proper attitude in life, for He bore our infirmities in His body and by His stripes we are healed.

Have you ever wondered about the relationship between the beginning of this passage and the end? What about the relationship between our reaction to offenses and healing? No one can be used to heal someone else while harboring evil in his heart. No one having evil desires toward another person can be used to take healing to others. If you feel prejudices towards certain people, how can God use you to touch them with His power? By the same token, how can God use someone to bless you if you harbor something against someone else in your heart? In order to minister in His power, it is vital to have a heart free of resentment toward others.

In order to minister in His power, it is vital to have a heart free of resentment toward others.

Anyone who responds with cursing cannot be used to bless others. Anyone who does that shows that he himself is fertile ground for bitterness and offenses. For that reason he cannot be used to heal others. Many do not receive more of the anointing because they harbor resentment against other people and have bitterness in their hearts. That is why they lose the honor of being an instrument of blessing unto others.

Jesus gave us an example of how we should behave when faced with criticism and offenses. He never returned the insults, curses or bad treatment that He received nor did He ever threaten to seek vengeance. We must follow His steps and learn from His character, humbling ourselves even when it seems so much easier to return evil for evil. Let us learn to suffer for doing what is good just as the Lord did in order for Him to bless us.

No child of God should harbor ill feelings toward anyone else. Learn to forgive if you want to be like Jesus. Do not assume that a healthy soul is one that has never had a grievance; on the contrary, the soul that has learned to react properly and manage its emotions toward grievances received is the soul that keeps itself healthy and whole. Offenses are capable of damaging your soul. However it is your decision and determination that allows them to do so. A former first lady of the United States named Eleanor Roosevelt once said: "No one can make you feel inferior without your consent." Being easily offended is a symptom of a weak soul that can withstand very little. It is not necessarily the evidence of a serious offense. Submit your heart to the discipline of the Lord and you will always be ready for the Lord to use you.

On one occasion, I was very badly hurt when some people who were close to me caused me a grave offense. Then, as always, I immediately prayed to forgive them but as the peace of the Lord began to fill me, I discovered that the Lord Himself was very angry about what they had done. I felt the assurance that He would act on my behalf if I asked Him to. My spirit knew that He would move His hand against them and I meditated on this. I understood then that I should raise a different prayer. I asked the Lord to take no action against them as He had planned and asked Him to let the offense go. Even though I knew that I could ask for justice or simply leave the matter of justice in His hands to carry out, I believed that was not the best thing for me. I wanted to grow in love, and I asked the Lord to show mercy to my aggressors. I acted this way to keep my heart at peace and to feel free of offense. I cannot minister in the anointing with a soul that desires vengeance.

Demons themselves try to use offenses to wear you down so that you will stop doing what is good. This is why you must forgive every offense you receive in prayer. Otherwise your soul will become sick and start desiring to repay evil for evil. There is no valid excuse when it is a matter of being used by God. You should maintain a healthy soul, and there is nothing more pleasant than living free of negative feelings against others.

Jesus is the bishop and guardian of your soul, and He wants to keep it healthy in order to use you. You should be a person who is able to look at others straight in the eye and never hold a grudge against them. Your manner of speaking will become more pleasant and your eyes will be filled with light when you are at peace. It will feel wonderful to raise your hands to God with a pure heart and say to Him: "Lord, please use me now!"

Managing Your Emotions

One night before a meeting, I bowed down in my room to pray and asked the Lord to heal the sick. In my eagerness for the Lord to move, I anxiously prayed that He might do something for those in need. And in the midst of my prayer, I said something like: "Lord, please heal them. Please, touch them Lord." The tone in my voice was that of desperation. My prayer was so full of agony and weeping that it was almost as if I were saying to God: "I am pleading with you in this way so that you will heal them." He interrupted me and said: "Why are you asking Me as if I don't want to heal them?" He wanted me to understand that He was more interested in healing the sick than I was. How else could He have borne our infirmities in His body and died on the cross? If He paid the price, it is because He is more interested in healing the sick than we are. So I began to thank the Lord for all the miracles that I would see. The following day the anointing was powerfully poured out and many people were healed and delivered.

We cannot ask God for a miracle when our attitudes tell Him that we do not believe that He wants to heal us.

We cannot ask God for a miracle when our attitudes tell Him that we do not believe that He wants to heal us. No one arrives at a large shopping center begging the shopkeepers to sell them something, nor does anyone enter his house crying for his wife to serve him supper. So why do we tend to beg God for things?

I have learned one important thing after so many years in the healing ministry. It does not matter how painful the infirmity might be, Jesus can perform a miracle and put a smile on the person's lips. He is not moved by the needs of people, but rather by faith. If the power of God were poured out because of pity for the needy, everyone would receive a miracle. But God is only moved by faith, because without faith it is impossible to please Him. When you pray in faith for the healing of a sick person, your emotions can sometimes deceive you. You must take charge of your emotions so that they do not attack your faith, which is the greatest capital you have.

On one occasion, I was ministering and the ushers brought me a child suffering from hydrocephalus so that I might pray for him. When they placed him before me, I was so moved that I started imagining his family's suffering. All I could do was weep. The shock of seeing this sick child was so great that my faith totally disappeared. When I was able to restore my composure and pray, nothing happened. Later the Lord reproved me, saying: "The sick do not need you to weep for them. They need you to believe with them." That was how I learned to manage my emotions so that I could be active in faith, in favor of those in need. They do not come looking for someone to feel sorry for them or to feel sorry about their sufferings. They are seeking someone who will declare the Word of faith for their healing.

Individuals who make constant use of their faith learn to recognize the moment when faith is flowing and when it stops. That is how we learn to manage not only our faith, but also the faith of those who come to us seeking prayer. On some occasions, when I pray for others, I ask them to look at me. I do that because I see that they have come forward to ask for a miracle, but they are more concerned about their sickness than about believing for their answer from God. They need someone to help them in their faith so they will not lose it. They need to see a ray of faith in the eyes of someone who can inspire them to believe that God will heal them. They do not need to recite their entire clinical history. They simply need the help of a pastor who can believe in a miracle with them.

The Lord Jesus also helped people conserve their faith. Jairus, a leader of the synagogue, begged Him to go to his house to pray for his twelve-year-old daughter who was sick. As the two were traveling along the road, in the midst of a multitude, a woman touched His garment wanting to be healed of an issue of blood. The Lord stopped to talk to her. At that moment some messengers arrived to tell Jairus not to trouble the Master anymore because his daughter had died. I imagine that Jairus' heart must have been completely broken when the news came to him and he must have felt much grief. The Lord immediately ministered to the emotion of fear that could have destroyed his faith. Jesus turned around and said to him: "Do not fear, just believe." He did not allow anyone else to follow Him except Peter, James and John, and when they arrived at the house He asked everyone else to leave the room. Taking the child by the hand, He told her to rise up, and she began to walk. Because the Lord helped Jairus to maintain his faith in the midst of all the adversities, He helped him experience the miracle that he so desired.

The Power of Honor

I recall once feeling quite ill. I had a really bad headache and I was in the convention center of a hotel on my way to the platform to preach. A brother from the church, well known for his strong personality, was walking beside me. When I told him that I was not feeling well, he told me that he would pray for me and that I would be healed. We stopped, he placed his hands on me and said in a firm voice: "Satan, I will not allow you to touch my pastor for he is a man of God. Leave him now in Jesus name." Later he added, turning toward me: "You are healed now!" That very moment I felt the power of God. If I had stopped to think about this man's character or about what others were saying about him, I would not have believed that God could use him that way. But I did not see his weakness. I saw the Son of God in him. I believed that the Lord could use him for a miracle, and the moment he prayed, I was healed!

Honoring God and the vessel He chooses is vital for miracles to flow through them. The Lord Jesus healed many times in different places. But in Nazareth, His hometown, He was unable to do any miracles, except for a few. Everyone in Nazareth saw Him merely as the son of a carpenter from whom they could expect a chair or a table. They did not see Him as the Son of God who could heal them. What you see in other people greatly determines what you are able to receive of them. The Holy Spirit moves where honor is given to God, not where there is criticism and murmuring. We live in a Kingdom and we need to learn to conduct ourselves as citizens of that Kingdom. That is why we should honor those who represent the Lord.

Honoring God and the vessel He chooses is vital for miracles to flow through them.

One of the most memorable miracle crusades we have ever organized was held in my hometown of Guatemala City in March of 2008. For two consecutive nights we packed our national soccer stadium, Mateo Flores, beyond capacity. There was no more room for all the people and many had to watch the crusade on some of the large screens we had mounted outside. We had to ask the people by radio to please stop coming. On the second night, we started two hours earlier than programmed, because the stadium was already full. Many secular radio stations supported the event and several pastor friends attended to offer assistance. It was a powerful event that left an unforgettable mark on our ministry and our city. It was the fulfillment of a dream that I had kept in my heart from the day that I surrendered my life to the Lord and asked Him to use me to bless my country, just as he had used many foreigners up to that time. But what really encouraged me was the attitude of the people who arrived by the thousands, breaking with the age-old proverb that no prophet is honored in His own country. The Lord manifested Himself powerfully and healed many people because He saw the honor they were demonstrating.

Some believe that God cannot use them with their family or in their country because they misinterpret the passage that says that a prophet is honored everywhere except in his own country. If you read the context you will see that the focus of this passage is not on your city or country of origin, but on the lack of honor. If the place of origin had been the problem, we would have to accept that in Mexico there cannot be any Mexican pastors or that in Guatemala there cannot be any Guatemalan pastors. Everyone called by God to minister would have to move to another country. The people of Nazareth did not believe that a carpenter from their city could heal them. They did not honor Him as the Son of God, and that is why they would not believe in the power of the Holy Spirit that rested upon Him. You can flow in the anointing in the place where you are respected and honored, whether it is in your family, neighborhood, workplace or university. God wants to use you to bless those who are nearest to you.

When God uses you, you should be careful with both pride and false humility. False humility seeks

In Honor of the Holy Spirit

the appearance of virtue by belittling one's self. The Lord Jesus never spoke negatively about Himself. He said: "I am the light of the world, whoever believes in Me will not walk in darkness," "I am the resurrection and the life, He that believes in Me will not die," "I am the Good Shepherd, for I lay down My life for the sheep." Time and time again we read His declarations: "I am the bread of life," "I am the door to the sheep-fold," "I am the true vine," "I am the way, the truth and the life." He spoke well of Himself, because He believed in His identity before God and the people. His humility did not keep Him from revealing who He really was. Do you know who you are?

Only when you recognize what God has given to you will you finally be able to give something to others. When you believe in who you are and what you have in the Lord, confess it to others so that they may believe also. Whenever I prepare to go out on the platform to minister at a crusade, the voice of the Lord gives me His affirmation. I hear the Holy Spirit reminding me: "You are my prince, go out and believe that they will be healed, and you will see it."

Believe as He does and you will see the Lord use you with His powerful anointing to bless countless people.

Believe as He does and you will see the Lord use you with His powerful anointing to bless countless people.

Chapter 12

Healing the Sick

One night many years ago, I had a dream that would mark the beginning of a powerful change in my ministry. I dreamed about an evangelist who was wonderfully used in healings and miracles, named Kathryn Kuhlman. She was well known internationally for the powerful manifestations that occurred during her divine healing crusades. In my dream, I saw that she had died and a person was calling me to deliver two boxes, saying: "She left these for you." I was confused, but I opened the boxes. The first contained books and more books. The other box was full of clothing. I remember feeling very surprised, taking an item out and saying, "How am I going to wear this?" Obviously, the clothing was a symbol of the mantle of anointing that I would receive, but I did not fully understand it at the moment.

Days later, a woman who we lovingly call Mama Rosa gave me a book by Kathryn Kuhlman entitled *Vislumbres de Gloria* [Glimpses of Glory]. The odd thing was that books by this preacher were not sold in any bookstore in my country, but she just happened to have one. Without knowing anything about my dream, she gave it to me. Soon after, two more books by the same author came to my hands. The message was clear.

While I was praying one night, the Lord told me that He would use me for miracles just as He had used Kathryn Kuhlman and that I would know when the time had arrived. I had always wanted to be used by God for divine healing. Since childhood I had been concerned for others' wellbeing and did not want anyone to get sick or to suffer. My mother remembers that when I was small I would give away my jackets to people on the street so they could cover themselves, even if it meant that I would be cold. When the Lord gave me this promise of healings and miracles in massive meetings, I was already visiting the sick in their homes and in hospitals. I had prayed and laid hands on people to be healed. But He wanted to do something that would have a greater impact. He wanted to give me an anointing to minister healing at huge meetings where many people could receive their miracle at the same time.

One day as I was ministering in a meeting, I experienced what I had long been waiting for. I felt His hand on my back and I saw His silhouette by my side. I understood that it was Him, and with great emotion I said: "Lord, You are by my side!" But He gently responded: "No, it is you who are by My side." I understood that He is the one who places us at His side. We do not place Him at our side. Later, I saw Him walking in the midst of the people and He said to me: "Declare My healing to the sick because this is their day." That very moment, with all the faith my heart could muster and with my strongest voice, I began to declare healing to the sick and the miracles began to happen. That was the first massive healing meeting in my life.

He Wants to Use You!

Many times people approach me to tell me that surely God will use me because I am a good person and I have a good heart. What they do not know is that, in a certain sense, He uses me because the people believe that He is going to use me. The same thing would happen if they believed this about themselves. Why not use your faith and believe that God can also use you? God wants to give you His power to heal those who are sick with cancer, who are paralyzed, who are blind and deaf. God can manifest Himself through anyone who deems himself worthy to be used by Him.

Why not use your faith and believe that God can also use you?

Do not think that your conduct has to be perfect for God to use you. Only Jesus, the Lamb of God who shed His blood on the cross to grant us eternal life, was ever perfect. It is not your conduct that gives you access to God, but the grace of our Lord Jesus Christ who was sacrificed for us. You have access to the throne of God thanks to Him, not thanks to you. It is in that grace that He wants to use you to show His power.

Do you believe that God can use you? You do not need to understand why He is using you, but you must believe that He will use you. When I see my defects and weaknesses, I thank God for His grace. I do not doubt or question, I simply believe that He can use me, not because I am perfect, but because He promised to do so. You are your own executioner if you condemn yourself for not being perfect, hindering God from using you. He cannot use you that way. His power, though, will flow through you if you believe that His grace can anoint you as you are.

We should see miracles every day and allow God to use us to perform them. I have seen God use children to perform miracles. I have seen young people dressed in t-shirts and fancy hairdos minister powerfully under the anointing of God. A new generation is flourishing because young people are believing in the presence of God and in His power. Someone could say that a child does not have the preparation to be an evangelist or that young people lack the maturity to minister under the anointing of the Holy Spirit. This just reflects their level of belief in God. He uses people who are simple and genuine and He longs to use you just as you are.

He uses people who are simple and genuine and He longs to use you just as you are.

Fulfilling His Orders

Healing the sick is more than a gift or a special ministry; it is a command that the Lord gave to all believers. It is our responsibility to pray for the sick without worrying about whether we have the gifts of divine healing or not. When you obey Him, the miracles will begin to follow you. Pray for the sick and don't wait on the Lord to do it for you. You are the one who should be healing them in the power of the Lord Jesus Christ. Look at what the Word of God says in Mark 6:12-13: "They went out and preached that people should repent. They drove out many demons and anointed many sick people with oil and healed them."

If you look carefully at this verse, you will notice that it was the disciples who healed them, not the Lord. They were the ones who went out preaching and casting out demons in Jesus' name, under the power of the Holy Spirit.

The disciples had assumed the responsibility that the Lord had delegated to them of praying for the sick, and they obeyed. That is why miracles followed them wherever they went. That same command also applies to you and to me. When you believe that you are the one who should be doing these things, you will begin to exercise your responsibility. Whoever fulfills it will see the power of God manifested in their life.

Jesus has already paid the price for miracles to occur; now He has given us the command to pray for the sick. By His stripes we are healed and it is our responsibility to lay hands on them and pray believing for it. You and He are one, and you work together for the healing of others. He commands you to do this in His name, because He has already paid the price.

When you pray for a sick person you must command them to receive healing. I remember that while ministering at a miracle meeting, I was praying for the sick in a general way and I gave a word of knowledge that the feet of a certain person were being straightened. Present at that meeting was a young person born with feet so twisted that the front parts of his feet were facing inward. This deformity made it difficult for him to jump and run the way his friends did. One of his dreams was to be able to play basketball, but his impediment created limitations. When he heard the word, he believed it, he bowed his head and looked at his feet, and with all the authority and determination he could produce, he pointed at his feet with his index finger and said, "That's for you, so straighten up right now." That very instant, before his own eyes, his feet began to straighten out. No one prayed for him. No one laid hands on him. He only believed the Word and ordered his feet to straighten out. That is exactly what happened. Those who know him told me later that this young man now plays basketball at his school. The same thing has happened with people suffering from flat feet. Several children and adults have testified that the moment I gave the Word, a curvature was formed on the soles of their feet.

Every time I go to a miracle meeting I know that I am representing the Lord. He is the one who sent me to perform miracles in His name. That is why I order the infirmity to disappear and the body to be made whole. When you pray or minister in the name of Jesus, you do so as His representative. It is not because you are perfect but rather because you believe in the authority that was delegated to you in Jesus' name. So when you go to pray for someone in the name of Jesus, do so knowing that it was He who sent you to do that work and His authority will always back you up.

Declare the Word

In Luke 5:17-26 we read the story of the paralytic who was lowered from the rooftop by four friends and placed before the Lord Jesus for healing. We see at the beginning of the story that the Lord was not praying for the sick but only teaching the people. We read: "One day Jesus was teaching, and Pharisees and teachers of the law were sitting there. They had come from every village of Galilee and from Judea and Jerusalem. And the power of the Lord was with Jesus to heal." (v. 17)

Notice that the Bible tells us that the power to heal was with Him, but He was not healing anyone at that moment. He was only instructing the Pharisees and the teachers of the law when suddenly He was interrupted by four men who tore through the roof of the house and lowered a paralytic on a cot. I imagine that some of the people present might have been troubled by the disorder that this must have caused. But Jesus stopped, looked at the man lying on his cot and glanced upwards at the friends so determined to get a miracle for him. They had not been deterred simply because the multitude would not allow them in. They believed their friend would be healed. So they made up their minds to bring him before Jesus any way they could. One of them must have gotten the idea of lifting the sick man onto the roof, opening a hole in the roof and lowering him into the house. Imagine the risk they were taking! But they believed, and overcame the obstacles through their faith. The Lord took notice of that, because faith always pleases Him. Anyone might have expected Him to perform a miracle immediately, but that is not what happened. Although He had a paralytic man in front of Him and the power was upon Him to heal, He did not heal him. Instead, He told him that his sins were forgiven. This upset the Pharisees and the teachers of the law, who thought that Jesus did not have the authority to forgive sins. So He asked them whether it was easier to tell this man that his sins were forgiven or to tell him to take up his bed and walk. No one answered, so the Lord broke the silence and declared the Word. When He did that, the man's body straightened and he stood to his feet in the presence of everyone there, took the bed which he had been lying on and started to walk home, giving glory to God. This man was healed because the Lord declared the Word and thus activated the healing power that was upon Him.

In your mouth there is power. You can use your words to declare healing with authority.

In your mouth there is power. You can use your words to declare healing with authority. Do not be confessing just your problems and the trials that you are going through. Declare that the promises of God will be fulfilled in your life as well. In this story, the Lord already had the power to heal, but it was not activated until He declared the Word. In the same way, the blessing of God may be with you, but it can only be activated when you confess it. When you believe the Word of God and declare it, mighty wonders will occur.

Praying for the Multitudes

Our first formal healing crusade began after some friends invited me to minister the presence of the Holy Spirit in Quito, Ecuador. In those meetings the manifestation of the power of God was so strong, that people were lying on the sidewalks outside the church completely filled with the Holy Spirit.

Among the leaders of the church was a young lady who was the daughter of another pastor of a very influential church in the city. This young lady was present during those evenings and decided to ask her father's permission to invite me to their church to minister there, too. Without my knowing it, she showed a video to her father of what had happened at the church where I had ministered, but the scenes did not show much of the manifestation of the power of God. She had chosen to show some scenes from a rather calm and uneventful night, and so her father granted her request. The pastor could not have imagined what was in store for him and to be honest, neither did I.

Several days later the invitation came to my office to go and minister there and the Holy Spirit led me to accept it. The meetings were glorious and the power of God was greatly poured out. The pastor and his family were powerfully touched by the outpouring of the Holy Spirit. What occurred was so strong that in my moments of prayer alone in the bedroom where I was staying, the Holy Spirit revealed to me specifically what he was going to do with the people, even giving me the names of many of them. After a week of ministry, the pastors testified that many sick people had been healed during the meetings. They were all so amazed at what was happening that they suggested I hold a series of healing meetings, calling them *Nights of Glory*. I was very moved, first by the miracles that had occurred and then because I had an opportunity to hold the first of those meetings that I had dreamt of since I was young.

The pastors suggested that we have them in the Rumiñahui Coliseum, which could hold about eighteen thousand people. When they took me there to see the venue it seemed so gigantic, and I asked myself: "What will I ever do to fill this place?" The next question was: "How will I pay for this?" Then they suggested that I invite some famous singer to help with gathering and bringing in the people, but I turned down the idea. My answer, in a somewhat joking tone, was: "We're going to do this without any tricks or gimmicks. Let those who are really hungry and thirsty for God and His Holy Spirit come, and if that is not the case, then they have no reason for being here."

We tried to do everything with excellence, using the best available sound system and lighting. This would be the first time we would use cameras to record the service. No one had advanced any money to pay for the crusade. As I explained earlier, this was the event for which we had decided to sell our house to cover the expenses. Of course, the Lord surprised us when we returned to our

187

country, because someone helped us by paying the difference that we were lacking.

The coliseum was full those entire three nights in May 1999. Fifteen thousand people received Jesus as their Savior during those meetings. During that first crusade I saw the blind recover their sight, people with limbs that were useless now able to move them, and, most amazing of all, a mentally ill person recovered and made whole. At the end, a woman approached me to say that everything had turned out nicely, but that we had committed one grave error which was spending too much money. I answered that if we were to compare the amount of money spent with the number of people who were saved and blessed, things had been very inexpensive indeed.

That is how I embarked on the adventure that soon became known as our *Nights of Glory* healing crusades. When we celebrated the tenth anniversary of those meetings, we did a review of what the Lord had allowed us to achieve in His loving-kindness. We realized that more than a million people had made a confession of faith during those meetings, and even many more had been healed. This could only be a product of God's faithfulness in fulfilling His promises.

I am believing for the day when all the sick people who attend a healing crusade will be healed, just as it was in Jesus' ministry. However, until that happens I rejoice with those who are being healed at every opportunity. When I finish ministering, I often have conflicting feelings. I get excited and emotional about those who received their miracle, but I cannot stop thinking about those who did not. It is sad to see many who travel great distances to come to a healing crusade and then go home without their miracle. It is painful and I intercede for them that the Lord might touch them on their way back, on the following day or at the next opportunity they have. I know that He longs to heal them.

Many ask why some are not healed and I really do not know. Others may offer some reasons, but I do not dare to offer any. I cannot judge those who are not healed by saying that they do not have faith, for they have already had enough pain to deal with and do not need anyone else to further condemn them. Our responsibility is to give hope, to motivate them to believe for their miracle. If it did not happen on that occasion, the Lord can do it the next day. They must say to themselves: "Today could be the day that I will receive the miracle I desire."

Our responsibility is to give hope, to motivate them to believe for their miracle.

But I cannot stop when I see so many others being healed. That is why I celebrate the victory, because each miracle proves that the Lord continues to do His work to this day. And this is why I am amazed and deeply moved every time I hear a testimony, so much that I cannot avoid laughing, jumping for joy, and singing to Him. This is why I promised the Lord that I would do everything possible to tell the world about the wonders He continues to do today.

On one occasion the Lord asked me: "Do you want to know why I use you the way I do?" I had never asked Him because I was not looking for reasons to glorify myself. I preferred to be used without knowing why, and to simply be thankful for His love. But on the day that God asked me this question, I asked Him for the

189

answer and He said: "Because what you do is directly related to My Son's sacrifice and I will always back that up, no matter what. You preach salvation, you minister healing and you teach my people to prosper. My Son paid for all of these things through His death."

God is present to do miracles. Ask Him to use you for His glory and honor, and He will do it. Ask for His support to do the work and you will soon see yourself doing great things for Him. Do not seek the limelight, only seek to serve. Do not seek fame, but if God gives it to you, use it to bring more people to Him. Do not seek money, but if God gives it to you, use it to reach more people and bless them. Go and do the work!

Closing Chapter

The Bicycle...or Me?

Many years ago, when we had recently started our church, I experienced a very intense moment. Within myself I was battling over some issues concerning my calling. It was then that I received a surprise call. It was a regular day, but I made an exception in my routine of taking our children to school and I decided to stay at home alone and pray. That very moment the phone rang.

I answered it and heard the voice of an older man who asked me: "Is this the servant of God, Cash Luna?" At first I was surprised at his greeting and I even thought to myself: "What kind of greeting is this?" repeating the same declaration that the Virgin Mary gave to the angel Gabriel. So I responded, "Yes, this is he." "The Lord says that he called you to preach His Gospel to the rich and the poor, to people who are academically prepared and to those who do not even know how to read and write. That in a few days you will be anointed as the kings and the priests were in the Old Testament."

Then I asked him who he was, but he did not want to give me his name. He only told me that he was a man of God and that he knew by the Spirit that I had been praying the night before, asking God for more definition in my life. He told me of specific things that I had been seeking, as if he had been present there during my prayer time. After this he hung up. I was amazed and grateful to God for giving me evidence of His faithfulness.

A week later he called again. Once again that particular day I had decided not to go with my wife to drop our children off at school. This time he told me that "the Lord was telling me not to hold back, but to lengthen the cords and stretch my tent curtains wide" (see Isaiah 54:2). This was precisely the same Word the Lord had called me with some time before. He added that God had spoken to him and told him to anoint me with oil, as a prophetic act of what was to come, because God was going to anoint me with His Spirit. He also told me that he was waiting to anoint my wife and me at a specific location in a neighborhood on the outskirts of the city, and then he gave me his name. It seemed strange to me because I knew that he was the administrator of a nursing home. But when I heard all the intimate details that he knew about my relationship with the Lord, I understood that God was definitely in the middle of all this, speaking through him by His Spirit.

So my wife and I prepared ourselves by fasting and kept our appointment at the scheduled time and day. The man came out to receive us. Wanting to call his attention to the strangeness of what he was planning to do, I said, "Excuse me, but why are you going to anoint me if you don't even know me? What if you are anointing someone who is no good?" Of course, I knew my own behavior and I was sure of my own integrity, so I did not say this for myself, but

I said this to avoid being anointed by someone who anoints haphazardly. The man responded with a tone of authority: "Look, I am already old and if there is something I have learned over the years, it is to hear God and obey Him. He told me to anoint you and that is what I'm going to do."

Then I thought to myself: "And why should I allow myself to be anointed by this man?" I did not want to fall prey to someone handing out random callings to others. But at that moment the Lord reminded me of the Word in Romans 12:16: "Do not be proud, but be willing to associate with people of low position." And then He added: "None of the great and renowned men are going to anoint you, so that you will always remember that it is I who did this and from where I raised you up." And I responded: "That's perfect, Lord. So be it. Anoint me."

This man washed our feet and then served us the Lord's Supper. Afterwards he placed some towels on the floor and told us to kneel on them and he took out an enormous jar of oil with spices, similar to the formula for the anointing oil that was used on priests in the Old Testament. At that moment, I imagined that he would put his hands in the oil and then place his hands on my head, as was the custom, or perhaps he would place a little anointing oil on my forehead or on my head, but that is totally not what happened. To our surprise, he poured out the entire container of oil over us, as if we were taking a bath. We were literally totally drenched in it. The oil was covering our heads, dripping down our face and shoulders, and getting into our eyes and our clothing. We were very touched and broken by the Lord. That day I could really feel the power of God in that place.

When we left I said to my wife that I wanted to take her for a cup of coffee at a Swiss café in the mall. My wife agreed but said that we should stop by our house to clean up and change clothes first, because we were literally dripping and smelling like oil. But I insisted that we go just like we were. When we arrived there, we sat down on one of the tables near the door, facing the aisle where everyone would walk by. There was so much oil on our heads that when I tried to take a sip of coffee, drops of it would fall into the cup. The people in the coffee shop who knew us were surprised to see us, but they did not say a thing. That moment I said to my wife: "I invited you to have coffee this way, dripping with oil, in front of all these people passing by us, because we will never be ashamed of His anointing or of what God is capable of doing."

We are living in a time when some of God's children and even ministers fear the manifestations of the Holy Spirit and the physical reactions that our bodies may experience. I wanted to be sure that nothing like that would ever happen in my heart. I do not presume to understand everything that God is doing, but in my heart I accept whatsoever comes from Him.

What my wife and I did that afternoon in front of everyone, with oil dripping from our heads, our hair all sticky and our clothing soaked, might have seemed embarrassing to some, even humiliating to others. But for me, to display the power of the Holy Spirit to the world is an honor. By His mercy, our television program is aired to millions of Latin American viewers. I do not believe that it is an accident that the Lord uses me to make known His wonders. Surely He must have seen that peculiar scene in the coffee shop and thought: "There is that son of mine who is not ashamed of Me or of My anointing. Let us raise him up and use him to spread My Gospel."

Do not be ashamed of the Holy Spirit, for He is never ashamed of you. Walk and have fellowship with

Do not be ashamed of the Holy Spirit, for He is never ashamed of you.

Him, testify of His works and you will always enjoy His company.

My Presence Will Always Be with You

Sometimes I find myself praying the same prayer that Moses prayed in the desert. When he asked the Lord who would accompany him to the Promised Land, God answered that His angel would go before them. But Moses told Him that he preferred staying in the desert to walking without His presence in the land of abundance. For him, the wilderness with God seemed better than a land that flowed with milk and honey, but without His presence.

When I was about to get married, I was still living in that small room where I learned to seek the presence of God and to have fellowship with His Spirit. I was still sleeping on the small cot loaned to me, and before moving to the house that I would share with Sonia, my wife, I asked the Lord to accompany me. I said that His presence was vital for me wherever I might go and that if He did not go with me, I preferred to stay there. Then I prayed one of those prayers that must have surely made Him laugh: "Lord, if You do not go with me, do not take me from here. So You are going to have to either make this bed larger or make Sonia smaller, because I am not leaving here without you." Of course, His presence went with us to our new home.

197

Every time a change occurs in my life and ministry, I pray the same prayer: "Lord, unless You go with me, do not take me from here." I prayed this when we moved to the house that we built and when the church dedicated our new building. If His presence does not accompany us, it would be of no use for me to do what I am doing, however good it might appear.

If His presence does not accompany us, it would be of no use for me to do what I am doing, however good it might appear.

The Bicycle or Me?

When as a child I had that encounter with the Lord in my bedroom that I described in earlier chapters, it had a great impact on me. From that moment on I began to hear a small voice in my heart that guided and confronted me.

I remember two instances in which He clearly spoke to me. One of them was concerning a bicycle that I wanted very much as a child. It was a California-style bike, in vogue at the time, a style that preceded the famous BMX model. I wanted a red one and I was very persistent, asking my mother every day so that she would get me one.

I remember one night, when I was going to sleep, that inner voice saying to me clearly: "Do you prefer the bicycle or Me?" I felt something indescribable in my stomach every time that voice spoke to me. It seemed to be churning, and the voice only repeated: "The bicycle or Me?" I answered: "You, Lord. It will always be You. If I have to choose between a bicycle or You, it will always be You, Lord." It might seem like an easy decision, but trust me it wasn't for a ten-year-old boy. But later, just as I had dreamt, I was given the bicycle, since all things are added unto us when we seek Him first.

The second instance that I remember has to do with some roller skates. At that time there were no in-line skates, only those with wheels attached to a metal frame which could then be attached to shoes and fastened with straps or hooks. The skates that I wanted had some edges for braking and a red plastic interior. They were the preferred brand because they did not damage the shoes or the soles. I was very eager to get myself a pair, and again I heard that voice asking me: "The skates or Me?" And I said: "You, Lord. It will always be You."

Years later, I was pastoring a church during the first few months after it was founded and we needed to find a larger venue to meet in. We rented a conference room at a hotel while believing God to prosper us so that we could get our own place. It was then that a businessman came along saying that God had told him to build a church precisely in the area where I wanted to have ours, and he came to talk to me about this. The church building was nearly complete and this man was looking for a pastor to whom he could donate the building. Can you imagine how happy I was? I was a young pastor who had recently started a church. I wanted to see miracles and I had faith that God would make the congregation prosper. It was easy to conclude that God had sent him. But here is the difference between just a person who draws conclusions based on signs and one who listens to the Lord.

This man attended one of our meetings the following Sunday. The power of God was being poured out in a mighty way and things that might seem strange to the eyes and natural, human mind were occurring. This man came from a very conservative church background and had been taught that these things should not happen in church, so he arrived and sat near the back. Suddenly a demonized young woman entered the place and was touched by the power of God. She fell to the floor and began to drag herself like a serpent, similar to incidents described in the Gospels of people who were later delivered. I was standing behind a wooden pulpit and when I turned around to see this man, he seemed very serious, with a disturbed look on his face. I thought of calming down the outpouring of the power of God to avoid the risk of him changing his mind and deciding not to give us the church building. However, doing so would have been at the expense of setting a young lady free!

At that moment I once again heard the voice from my childhood asking me to choose between the bicycle and Him. I literally felt as if a hand was placed on my chest and the voice was saying to me: "The church or Me," and I answered: "You Lord. Whenever You make me choose, You know that my choice will always be You. Above and beyond any material blessing, I will always choose You."

Obviously, they did not give me the church building because I did not stop the manifestation of the power of God. Incidentally, years later we built a church with capacity for 3,500 people in that same area of the city. We built it free of debt and without any bank loans. It was inaugurated in 2001 and now, in 2011, we are building a sanctuary for over twelve thousand people, as well as classrooms for twenty-eight hundred children and parking spaces for thirty-six hundred vehicles, all in an area of approximately eighty acres or forty city blocks.

When I chose the Lord, I lost the donation of a church building, but since then He has allowed me to build two larger ones. His blessings will always follow you as long as you choose Him above everything else.

His blessings will always follow you as long as you choose Him above everything else.

He has given us a wonderful promise: "His presence will always go with us." If one day you must choose between your fellowship with Him and one of His blessings, large or small, always choose Him just as He chose you. Never exchange Him for any of your dreams or desires no matter how beautiful they may seem, not even for a red California-style bicycle.

Remember: He is someone, not something.

We want to hear from you.
Please send your comments about this book to:

Vida@zondervan.com
www.editorialvida.com

THANK YOU.